Free Agents ©

*How America Moves from
Tea Parties to Real Change*

David Zanotti

First published in 2010 by
THE AMERICAN POLICY ROUNDTABLE / FREEDOM
FORUM
11288 Alameda Drive
Strongsville, Ohio 44149

ISBN: 978-0-97779632-3-2

Table of Contents

Free Agents ©

Introduction

This book is different. It is written from the experiences of people who actually do something about politics in America – not just talk about it. The original goal for this work was an addendum to *God Won't Vote This Year* originally published in 2007. As the work grew, however, many people requested we publish this as a separate work. In this brief book you will find a specific plan describing how you can make a positive, long-term impact in the arena of civil government.

One important disclaimer must be spelled out here. If you want to be famous, please don't waste your time reading this book. The conversation here is about changing America through a long-lost virtue called public service for the common good. If you get famous in the process we apologize. That was not our intention.

If "We the People" finally figure this out – if we finally get over our fears and phobias and move from protest to leadership, this nation can truly change.

Franklin, Tennessee
December 1, 2009

Free Agents ©

Chapter 1: What They Have Done to Your Country

In the summer of 2009 the media had a lot of fun covering town halls and tea parties. The meetings were "controversial" which is always good for TV footage. As long as there is not a fire, mass murder, or TV celebrity story to cover, controversial political meetings will make the news. So these high volume-shouting matches got a lot of coverage on television news and talk radio. The media covered the events but no one took the time to find out why people were so angry. In typical fashion, the media missed the real story and chose to spin the summer of 2009 into a battle between the Obama administration and Republicans. Nothing could be farther from the truth. The left side of the media tried hard to find non-attractive people and ugly moments to portray the heat of the summer of 2009. They were particularly fond of the stereotypical, overweight white person shouting about wanting their country back.

When people express their outrage over "losing their country" they are using the wrong words attempting to make a very important point. Something has changed in America. There is something desperately wrong in our government. The rhetoric of the town halls didn't quite get to the root of the problem but people sure were trying hard.

In the last half of the 20th century several major changes took place that radically altered the historic patterns of American governance. We feel the impact of these changes today, even if we are unaware of what actually happened. In brief summary, here are the key points where America jumped the tracks:

• We stopped teaching the basics of American history and government to our children. Parents stopped taking primary responsibility for this transfer of leadership. Churches and schools dropped the ball.

• We abandoned the self-evident truths, the Creator, and the biblical principles infused in the Declaration and Constitution. We substituted government as the source of human rights instead of the Creator.

• Congress expanded the responsibilities of the federal government far beyond the original constitutional design.

• The Federal Courts also expanded their role and began to compete with the legislative branch by making public policy decisions from the bench.

• The size of the federal budgets and state budgets grew so huge, so quickly that Congress and Statehouses became almost magical in their financial appeal. Gaining and keeping control over all that money and all those government jobs became the top priority for politicians and their allies.

• The Republican and Democrat parties morphed into competing corporations with a single purpose: gain control of the trillions in government spending.

All the people standing in line to benefit from all that spending were more than willing to care for any members in Congress or state government that could be counted on as friends. Thus the "lobbying" class joined the ranks of the ruling class as a type of security force. It doesn't matter whether they work for a luxury industry or the janitors union; the lobbying class provides the protection money the politicians need to keep their day jobs. They pass most of their obscene budget measures late at night.

In essence, "We the People," let our civil government become the kind of bureaucratic, tax-consuming, monstrosity that the founding generation would have gone to war to destroy. It took a while for the radical changes to happen but it did not take long for the tragic harvest. A person, born in 1925, who lived through the Great Depression, fought through World War II and survived the Cold War, saw all these changes happen. In the span of that lifetime a whole generation of Americans became the economic slaves to an elitist ruling government class. If those words sound too harsh, consider this: In 1948 the average American working family paid about 2% of their income in taxes to the federal government. What are you paying in taxes today?

Americans are the most fortunate people on earth, but with that fortune comes a danger. We are prone to a malignancy unique to the American experience. Most of us are handed ownership in this remarkable nation just because we were born here. Since our citizenship cost us nothing we tend to think the price of maintaining it is the same. We think no one could ever take our freedoms away. Like "trust fund babies" we have no real sense of the value of what we were given at birth. Somebody else paid so we could be free and we act that way.

If America was ever anybody's country, it belonged to the people who paid for its construction with their very lives. They are called the founding generation for a reason. For a long time their offspring kept fighting to prove themselves worthy of the gift of liberty. They fought to overcome slavery and injustice. They fought to bring civil rights to all citizens.

They fought through a great depression and battled dictators bent on America's destruction. It is their country that we, their historic offspring, have inherited just by being here. Sadly it is their country we have thrown on the trash heap of our modern illusions, addictions and neglect. "We the People" with this book in our hands are the generation that bears the responsibility for America as we find her today. We permitted this to happen. So rather than shouting protests for a television camera perhaps we should start by looking in the mirror.

Chapter 2:
The Great Divide

America has overcome many dangerous external enemies over the years but the greatest threats to liberty have always come from within. Today there is no question that America is divided into two classes of people. The division is not based on race, creed, color, or income. The division is between those who are in political power or are directly wired in to that power, and all the rest of us. America is divided between a government class and "We the People" who remain outside that circle of power. These two people groups are now moving toward a season of serious conflict.

No greater example could be seen of this great divide than the economic collapse that began in 2008. The truth about the banking or "Wall Street" collapse is that it was an inside job. The collusion of the power brokers in Congress and their allies at Freddie Mac and Fannie Mae working in harmony with Wall Street all came crashing down – on the "little people." The entire bubble was built courtesy of the ruling Congressional class and their pals on Wall Street and when it blew up, they handed the bill to the U.S. taxpayers. Did any of the culprits go to jail? Did any members of Congress lose their jobs like the millions of "little people" who suffered through the great recession?

During that time period unemployment soared in almost every sector of the economy but one – government jobs. How could that be? Because the members of the ruling class rang up trillions in new debt and created government programs to spend the money in the name of saving the economy. But did all those trillions in new debt and the following taxes save the American economy or simply increase the wealth, power and permanence of the ruling class?

If you worked in Washington you would see this great divide. Most everyone who lives and works in that community believes Washington, D.C. is the center of universal power. Even the taxicab drivers in D.C. carry the attitude that they are making history every day. It used to be called Potomac Fever. That malady was once treatable by a long trip back to the real world and some home cooking. Today, the members of Congress rarely see the place they once called home. Potomac fever for most is a life-long affliction.

This is a sad and deeply regrettable confession. The culture of Washington, D.C. is way past broken. It is now openly hostile to the everyday working American regardless of race, income or even political persuasion. I have heard Congressional staffers talking about "the people" back in the district. We have seen the ruling elites responses to town hall meetings and tea parties. It feels like we have reached the place where representative government is a distant memory. We now have lords of the manor and everyone else (the serfs). If you are not an elected official, or work for one, or have a job they create and control, then you simply are boring at best. To quote one famous Congressman, talking to you is as interesting as talking to "a dining room table."

It didn't used to be this way. There was a time when Congressional offices rolled out the red carpet if people from back home showed up on Capitol Hill. Visitors would look for their Congressman's office by finding their state flag in the hallway near the office door. The local folks were treated as special guests – after all, they were the reason the members of Congress and their staffs were in office in the first place.

Try visiting your U.S. Capitol, long known as "the people's House," today. Without special permission or a special tour you cannot even get in the building. You can go to an underground "Welcome Center" but you cannot walk up the steps and enter your Capitol as in days of old. You will be met with armed guards carrying assault weapons. Of course all this is blamed on 9.11 and terrorism. Are we really so sure?

If you are willing to endure the metal detectors you can get into the House or Senate Office buildings. These massive structures line Capitol Hill. But once you get inside, try getting an appointment with any of your members of Congress. Try getting past any of their layers of staff who insulate the members from "We the People." Try getting a member of Congress to return a letter or take your phone call. You will get a mailbox full of form letters that may remotely deal with your issues or concerns, but try getting an honest dialogue of any kind.

So should we be surprised when people start shouting at town hall meetings when one of the elite ruling class finally shows up? Should we be shocked when the crowd gets unruly when somebody they elected stands behind the podium and makes a speech to the media as if the people in the room don't even exist? When members of Congress will no longer even answer or take a direct question from their own constituents should we be surprised that people are angry?

How stupid do they think "the American people" really are?

Chapter 3:
The Truth About
Term Limits

Back in the early 1990s a bunch of unknowns found each other in a common mission. A few people started talking about term limits for politicians. The idea bounced around conservative and libertarian circles and found allies among a handful of entrepreneurs who were not owned by any of the political parties. The money people started looking for people on the ground that had real world political experience. They met up with a few reformers in the media who began beating the drum and soon an organic American movement was born.

I ran into term limits in the political journals of the day. My first response was to look at the U.S. Constitution. Since term limits were not originally found there, my first thought was they must not be necessary. Yes, the Constitution limits the terms of the President but that was because FDR went out of control and kept running (and winning) the Presidency. After dying rather scandalously in the arms of his mistress, the Roosevelt mystique began to wear thin. People realized they had made a mistake to permit one man the control of the Executive Branch for more than two-terms; so the Congress passed term limits on the President and the states ratified the amendment. That is where the matter stopped for two generations.

Further research revealed that term limits were discussed in the founding era and even considered for the federal constitution. The reason they were not added to the Constitution was clear in the record of history. The founding generation did not foresee a time when serving in the U.S. Congress would ever be viewed as a career path. They could not imagine a day when the size and scope of the federal government would afford members of Congress a lifestyle and income far superior to working for a living. Nor could they fathom the possibility of an electorate that would tolerate such a career Congress for long.

No President prior to Roosevelt broke the tradition established by George Washington who voluntarily walked away from the Presidency after two terms in office. He could have easily been re-elected for the rest of his life. Arguably, America might have been better served by a third Washington term compared to the administration of John Adams, our second president. This is no knock on Adams, one of the greatest American thinkers and true patriots. It's just that no one could possibly follow the legendary Washington and do well. Washington was just that huge of a personality in the American psyche. No President has ever lived up to Washington's stature. His farewell address is read on the floor of the Senate each year on his birthday. In 2010 no Senators chose to sit in the chamber to hear the reading.

Washington anchored the philosophy, practice, and tradition of term limits or voluntary rotation of office. The idea is that this government "of the people" should involve "We the People" in actual public service. There was to be no ruling class or elitist group who would control the constitutional republic. The only positions granted for life were in the federal judiciary but even there, Congress retained authority to impeach bad judges and limit the size and jurisdiction of the courts.

So in the early 1990s it took a lot to shake constitutionalists and traditionalists out of their comfort zones and into the movement to pass term limits on the legislative branch. For many people the tipping point came with the revelations of the House Bank and Post Office. My personal tipping point preceded those blockbuster scandals.

One day I was invited to visit the U.S. Capitol with a friend who had a close relative very highly placed in the infrastructure of Congress. This "cousin" was a very big wheel on the Hill. For a day we travelled the Capitol as few people do. There was no elevator we could not ride, no hallway we could not enter. The "cousin" seemed to know everyone and everyone knew him. He took us to the underground tunnels where members of Congress do their walking, talking and travelling. Along the way we were privileged to hear conversations about lots of "arrangements." There were tickets to the big games secured, events set-up with the White House, even baby-sitters arranged, all on the fly as the "cousin" moved from office to office. Messages were passed and delivered in a non-stop code of winks, nods, and handshakes. Back in his office he introduced us to members of his staff, who all seemed to be close relatives of major sports figures, entertainers, and powerful people. By the end of the day we were exhausted. I am certain our host thought he had shown us a good time and made a powerful impression. We couldn't wait to find a shower.

A few years later, many of the people we met that day were running from reporters and cameras. Somebody, somewhere, caught wind of internal networking of the House Post Office and Bank. Yes, Congress had its own little money laundering scam going on right inside the Capitol. Republicans and Democrats alike were kiting checks, trading postage stamps and campaign funds, and generally living as if they had their own little underground empire. Somehow, somebody found out. We were NOT the ones who blew the whistle but somebody did. Our experience led us in a different direction. It was that day on Capitol Hill that finally convinced us that General George Washington would either be mounting an army to attack the Congress or working to pass term limits. We chose option B.

The original groups that came together in multiple states worked to limit terms on their state elected officials AND members of Congress. Most of the states that passed term limits in the early '90s passed measures including Congressional terms. These measures were tried in Federal Court. The state provisions remained but the Supreme Court, in a bitterly divided decision, struck down the right of citizens to limit the terms of their Congressional representatives. The majority on the Court told the American people only Congress can limit Congress. An amendment would have to come forth from the Congress requiring a supermajority vote of both House and Senate then move to the states for ratification. Term limits for Congress died with that decision and the Courts sent Congress this clear message: "You are untouchable."

The Supreme Court decision was not really surprising. It took years for many of us to finally come to a place of supporting term limits. By the time we gathered millions of signatures, been rained on, punched around at the polls, castigated by the media, and called lots of names, we really were not surprised to be abused by the Supreme Court. Call it cynical if you like, but after years of challenging the establishment and calling for a return to a genuine citizen legislature we were not all that surprised that the U.S. Supreme Court would have none of it. After all, the entire federal bench is appointed for life by the President and approved for office by the Congress. Why would those with the coziest jobs in the world bite the hand that feeds them?

The truth about term limits is: it almost worked. States that have term limits in effect on their state legislatures are experiencing a better practice of government. The opportunities afforded by reasonable, balanced term limits legislation have made a way for new people to come into public service. True, some of the career politicians have found a way to bounce back and forth between jobs in the House and Senate, but they still cannot stay in the same job and build seniority and power for a lifetime.

For a brief moment it looked like the momentum of term limits would carry the day on Capitol Hill. Back in 1994, in response to the overwhelming success of term limits in the states, the Republicans swept back into power in Congress capturing the House. The new Speaker, Newt Gingrich, made lots of promises to bring forward a term limits amendment to the U.S. Constitution and give the states the right to do what the courts had denied them. That promise never materialized. Within a few years Gingrich, was drummed out of Washington due to corruption and scandals and the establishment career politicians quickly threw term limits to the curb.

For one brief moment in the mid-'90s it looked like Americans had a chance to break the stranglehold of the elitist ruling class on Capitol Hill. Term limits would have re-wired the internal plumbing of Congress. It would have upended the good old boy network that rewards party and personal loyalty over principle – always. It would have broken the power of the K-Street lobbying crowd or at least forced them to buy a new set of friends every six or eight years.

When the Republicans and Democrats in Congress combined to kill term limits they planted the seeds of the revolution that erupted in the summer of 2009. Americans have come face to face with reality. There are two classes of people in this country: those who hold and control power, and those who pay the bills for those in power.

A house so divided cannot stand.

Chapter 4:
It Wasn't Supposed to
Be This Way

Americans have always been at their best when challenged by outside enemies. When the nation began the colonists were united in a bitter struggle against Great Britain. After an eight year war the settlement for peace barely secured the new nation. American leaders knew their chances of survival were slim. They were the new kid in the world. Spain, England and France were at the doorstep, literally surrounding the colonies on the North American continent. The courts of Europe were placing strong odds against the fledgling rebels in America surviving for even ten years.

There was strong cause for such skepticism. The colonies were a loose-knit confederation at best, united by a rather sketchy document and governed by a voluntary Congress. There was barely an official federal government at the time. It was 13 colonies and their voluntary Congress against the world.

Can you imagine John Adams in the courts of Europe representing these 13 rebel states? That was his job: to represent the Continental Congress and settle the remaining issues of the peace settlement with England. There was no President, no constitution, no court system, and no national treasury of any substance.

So the leaders of the colonies had a decision to make. Would they stay independent sovereign states and build their independent empires or would they construct a stronger form of centralized government? They obviously took the second option. The proposals and debates over how they decided to construct that form of government remain with us today.

One of the primary reasons they chose to unite in a national form of government was survival. They united as a defense mechanism, first against Great Britain and then against the world. That essential unity against a common threat kept the colonies focused for a founding generation. They genuinely worked to put country first. They had bought the right to do so with their blood. Such sacrifices set the priorities and the culture of the Constitutional Convention and the new government.

It is critical that we understand this cultural reality of the founding period. The price that was paid for liberty and the huge risk of failure as a new nation forced a high level of accountability in civil government. People did not go to Congress to make a career. They went to work in a hot muggy or freezing cold Philadelphia. They left their families and travelled by horseback, not knowing if they would return to homes ravaged by small pox or if they would stay healthy enough to return home at all. Public service was not a game played for fame or a career path. It was a sacred duty for the sake of survival. And it was not fun or financially rewarding.

What an amazing contrast to the Congress of the 21st century. The differences are so sadly obvious that they need not even be stated except for one glaring omission. The first years of the American Republic were conducted without the existence of political parties. There was no provision for such entities in federal or state law. There was no consideration of legitimizing such an activity. In fact, the notion of creating and sustaining organized factions or parties was summarily condemned by America's first two Presidents: George Washington and John Adams.

Yes, from the beginning, there was a dividing fault line in America over the proper role of the federal government versus the authority of the sovereign states. This dividing line, however, was not strong enough to prevent the creation of the Constitution. Nor did it stop the goodwill found in the Northwest Ordinance where major land-holding states ceded (gave away) their rights to massive land tracts so new states could be developed. Most importantly the fault line between federalists (those advocating a strong national government) and those advocating stronger states rights was insufficient to generate the creation of any political parties until the third presidential administration.

The first two presidents wholly condemned political parties or factions. Their remarks are indicative of how the founding generations truly viewed civil government. They understood the government to be an agency of service for the common good, not a corporation to be controlled by warring parties. Let the record of their remarks speak for itself:

John Adams considered political parties: *"the greatest political evil under our Constitution."* His greatest fear was *"a division of the republic into two great parties, each arranged under its leader, and concerting measures in opposition to each other."* (Source: Official web site of the U.S. Senate)

George Washington said this in his Farewell Address:
I have already intimated to you the danger of parties in the

state, with particular reference to the founding of them on geographical discriminations. Let me now take a more comprehensive view, and warn you in the most solemn manner against the baneful effects of the spirit of party, generally.

This spirit, unfortunately, is inseparable from our nature, having its root in the strongest passions of the human mind. It exists under different shapes in all governments, more or less stifled, controlled, or repressed; but, in those of the popular form, it is seen in its greatest rankness, and is truly their worst enemy.

The alternate domination of one faction over another, sharpened by the spirit of revenge, natural to party dissension, which in different ages and countries has perpetrated the most horrid enormities, is itself a frightful despotism. But this leads at length to a more formal and permanent despotism. The disorders and miseries, which result, gradually incline the minds of men to seek security and repose in the absolute power of an individual; and sooner or later the chief of some prevailing faction, more able or more fortunate than his competitors, turns this disposition to the purposes of his own elevation, on the ruins of Public Liberty.

Without looking forward to an extremity of this kind, (which nevertheless ought not to be entirely out of sight,) the common and continual mischiefs of the spirit of party are sufficient to make it the interest and duty of a wise people to discourage and restrain it.

It serves always to distract the Public Councils, and enfeeble the Public Administration. It agitates the Community with ill-founded jealousies and false alarms; kindles the animosity of one part against another, foments occasionally riot and insurrection. It opens the door to foreign influence and corruption, which find a facilitated access to the government itself through the channels of party passions. Thus the policy and the will of one country are subjected to the policy and will of another.

There is an opinion, that parties in free countries are useful checks upon the administration of the Government, and serve to keep alive the spirit of Liberty. This within certain limits is probably true; and in Governments of a Monarchical cast, Patriotism may look with indulgence, if not with favor, upon the spirit of party. But in those of the popular character, in Governments purely elective, it is a spirit not to be encouraged. From their natural tendency, it is certain there will always be enough of that spirit for every salutary purpose. And, there being constant danger of excess, the effort ought to be, by force of public opinion, to mitigate and assuage it. A fire not to be quenched, it demands a uniform vigilance to prevent its bursting into a flame, lest, instead of warming, it should consume.

Chapter 5:

"Party Building" vs. Building America

On Tuesday, October 27th, 2009 Newt Gingrich had a conversation on FOX news. He spoke with commentator Greta Van Susteren regarding the Congressional race in New York's 23rd district. The conversation was actually more of a lecture by the former Speaker of the House to the people of America. Here is the exact transcript from the FOX website:

VAN SUSTEREN: Well, I look forward to her response to that because I'm sure she's going to get a lot of heat for that one. All right, the 23rd congressional district in New York -- you're getting heat from Glenn Beck and others because you have endorsed the Republican candidate, and many Republicans, like Tim Pawlenty, former governor Sarah Palin -- Governor Pawlenty, former governor Sarah Palin, Steve Forbes, Dick

Armey -- they've all endorsed the independent, and you're getting heat.

GINGRICH: Sure.

VAN SUSTEREN: And?

GINGRICH: Well, I just find it fascinating that my many friends who claim to be against Washington having too much power, they claim to be in favor of the 10th Amendment giving states back their rights, they claim to favor local control and local authority, now they suddenly get local control and local authority in upstate New York, they don't like the outcome.

There were four Republican meetings. In all four meetings, State Representative Dede Scozzafava came in first. In all four meetings, Mr. Hoffman, the independent, came in either last or certainly not in the top three. He doesn't live in the district. Dede Scozzafava...

VAN SUSTEREN: He doesn't live in the district?

GINGRICH: No, he lives outside of the district. Dede Scozzafava is endorsed by the National Rifle Association for her 2nd Amendment position, has signed the no tax increase pledge, voted against the Democratic governor's big-spending budget, is against the cap-and-trade tax increase on energy, is against the Obama health plan, and will vote for John Boehner, rather than Nancy Pelosi, to be Speaker.

Now, that's adequately conservative in an upstate New York district. And on other issues, she's about where the former Republican, McHugh, was. So I say to my many conservative friends who suddenly decided that whether they're from Minnesota or Alaska or Texas, they know more than the upstate New York Republicans? I don't think so. And I don't think it's a good precedent. And I think if this third party candidate takes away just enough votes to elect the Democrat, then we will have strengthened Nancy Pelosi by the divisiveness. We will not have strengthened the conservative movement.

VAN SUSTEREN: What is it that they have identified as why they think the independent candidate...

GINGRICH: Well, there's no question, on social policy, she's a liberal Republican.

VAN SUSTEREN: On such as abortion?

GINGRICH: On such as abortion, gay marriage, which means that she's about where Rudy Giuliani was when he became mayor. And yet Rudy Giuliani was a great mayor.

And so this idea that we're suddenly going to establish litmus tests, and all across the country, we're going to purge the party of anybody who doesn't agree with us 100 percent -- that guarantees Obama's reelection. That guarantees Pelosi is Speaker for life. I mean, I think that is a very destructive model for the Republican Party.

VAN SUSTEREN: It's sort of interesting, the names, especially former governor Sarah Palin and current governor Tim Pawlenty are sort of names that are batted around for 2012. Is this sort of positioning or moving into position, or not?

GINGRICH: Look, I have no idea. I think in the case of Governor Palin, she's clearly part of the conservative movement in a very national kind of way. The conservative movement has gotten very excited about this race, I think largely on misinformation. I think if people looked at this issue of local leadership, local control, local involvement -- the money raised in the district is overwhelmingly going to Dede Scozzafava and is not going to the independent candidate. He's getting his money from outside the district and mostly outside the state.

The fact is that on local issues, she actually knows what she's doing. He's said publicly he doesn't know what he's doing. And so you have to ask a question. If we're going to have representative government, aren't the people of upstate New York allowed to pick their candidate? In the polling data, she's clearly carrying Republicans.

(Source: Fox News, http://www.foxnews.com)

On Saturday morning, October 31st, Dede Scozzafava withdrew from the race for the 23rd district of New York. Her support in public opinion polls from the 23rd district had collapsed. She was running a distant third to the Democrat and Conservative candidates.

Newt Gingrich's lecture didn't stop the people from upstate New York from exercising their rights. The people didn't like the liberal Republican and chose not to support her in spite of what the party bosses from Washington and the cable empires tried to force them to do.

Doug Hoffman did not win the race. He lost by a razor-thin margin, thanks to Dede Scozzafava who threw her remaining support to the liberal Democrat candidate. Ever notice how leftist Republicans always chastise conservatives and independents for not being "team" players but seldom play team ball themselves?

The New York 23 race in 2009 is a case study exposing big name Republicans who would rather lose an election than permit conservatives a fair shot at holding office. If faced with standing with a solid conservative who might lose or picking a left-winger who might win, principle flies out the window. Instead of picking the conservative and urging all his party to get behind the nominee, Gingrich supported the liberal and then condemned conservatives for being selfish and not seeing the big picture. When faced with a tough call the national Republicans, almost always default to the left.

In late January 2010, former Speaker Gingrich visited New Hampshire. He admitted in an interview that his endorsement of Dede Scozzafava was "probably" a mistake. Gingrich defined himself as a "party builder" and admitted he was unaware how radical Scozzafava's positions really were. This is quite a remarkable admission, especially considering how Gingrich lectured the nation on how wrong the independents and conservatives were to support Doug Hoffman.

In 2004 Republicans pulled a stunt that should go down in history as the proof text for this failed strategy of always defaulting left for the sake of "party building." After years of insulting Republicans, defying party platforms and telling the voters of Pennsylvania to go pound salt, Arlen Specter faced re-election for the U.S. Senate. Conservative Republican Pat Toomey challenged Specter in the primary election. Toomey was a qualified candidate who could have beaten Specter and won in the general election. The Republican leadership faced a golden opportunity to get rid of a real problem and send a message to the nation. Even if Toomey failed to win the general election, Republicans would have been no worse off because Specter was and remains a devoted leftist. They couldn't count on his vote in the Senate anyway.

Instead of having the courage to back Toomey the Republican leaders fell back to the pathetic partisanship of the good-old boy era. They told the world they had to protect their incumbent Senator – no matter what. Loyalty to party was the political absolute. In the closing weeks of the primary President George W. Bush came to Pennsylvania to campaign for Specter. Even worse, the darling of the conservative movement at the time, U.S. Senator Rick Santorum, played party politics and campaigned for his fellow Senator, Arlen Specter. Toomey was defeated. Specter won re-election and a few years later betrayed his party and the voters of Pennsylvania and switched parties to join the Democrats.

Case closed.

Chapter 6:
Life After the Parties

There is a better way to do this. There is a way to get back to first principles without starting a third political party or tearing the nation apart. The first step is dealing with the false claims that America cannot survive without a two-color map.

We have already seen that America was not designed to be a bipolar entity split between two political parties. The founders never bought into that model. Furthermore, there have been several periods in history where three or more political parties or groups were dominant on the national scene. The current Republican Party (and they hate being forced to admit this) began as a third party. Abraham Lincoln was a third party candidate in a four-party race for the White House in 1860. How can the current Republican leaders or talk show hosts condemn people who want outside the box of a two-party dictated system? Would these same people have trashed the efforts of Abraham Lincoln?

As fun as that argument is to win, it is pointless to a degree. America doesn't need a third political party, especially when the first two are so dysfunctional. Most people want nothing to do with the Democrats or Republicans. They may be forced by state laws (passed by party players) to declare for a party so they can vote in a primary but that does not make them a "member" of anything. They don't go to party meetings, vote for party leaders or give a dime to either party.

Take a look at a few key states. In Florida over 25% of the voters are independent of any political party. In Massachusetts 51% of voters are non-aligned independents. In Ohio almost 60% of voters are independents. The trend is huge and growing across the nation. Most voters are done with party affiliations because the parties offer them nothing, assume their support, presume upon their time by assaulting them with endless fundraising letters and calls and do NOTHING in return. Bottom line – there is likely no one in the entire nation who has "joining a political party" ranked number one on their "to do" list.

So why does this two-party fantasy continue to dominate the media? Simply because newspapers and old-line media have always done business this way and they have no intention of changing now. Everything in their world is divided into two sets of files. The idea of having to get outside the box and find out what is new and exciting on the streets is way too much work for journalists who are used to being served by the party-owned media consultants.

Media owners are not risk-takers. They don't like to lose in public and they especially don't want to cover upstart politicians who challenge the status quo. Publishers and editorial boards cannot afford to tick off the establishment players for fear of losing access to the channels of power. If a paper or news network challenges an incumbent politician there is almost always payback. That media company will be denied access by the politicians and their staffs. So the media is trapped inside the two-party illusion.

For years the rising tide of independent voters in Massachusetts was under-reported by the mainstream media. Everyone was led to believe Massachusetts was a totally liberal state dominated by Democrats. Romney being elected Governor there was largely ignored or considered an anomaly based on Romney's wealth. Nobody reported that 51% of voters in Massachusetts were not Republicans or Democrats but independents. That fact only came to light when Scott Brown shocked the world and won a special election to the U.S. Senate in January 2010.

The point is – the change has already happened. More

Americans are now outside the two party "system" than are locked inside. Isn't it time we simply begin telling the truth? The political parties are dinosaurs facing a new ice age. Nobody needs them, few people want them, and fewer care – except the people who make a lot of money catering to the illusion of the status quo.

But independents are not allowed to run on most ballots, right? Don't candidates have to be Democrats or Republicans?

Wrong. Running for public office is a basic civil right in this country, not subject to the dictates of partisan political parties. In some states the laws require independents to jump through more or different hoops (thanks again to partisan lawmakers), but no state can keep a person off the ballot who is willing to follow the basic rules.

But independents can't run and win against the party machines, can they? Maybe we should ask Jesse Ventura who became Governor of Minnesota. Granted, his administration didn't make or keep many friends, but he got elected Governor in a big state as an independent. Ask Scott Brown how he got elected to the U.S. Senate? His answer is simple and straightforward. The independent voters in Massachusetts elected him to the Senate. Of course independents can run and win elections, provided they are quality candidates and run competitive campaigns.

Ah, but there is the catch – independents cannot possibly compete against the Democrat and Republican money machines, right? Who says they have to have more money to win? This is one of the greatest myths in American politics propagated largely by professional consultants who make millions raising and spending campaign funds. They want you to believe you can never beat a candidate with big money so you will not run. Campaign war chests are raised first and foremost to intimidate challengers from entering the race.

But how much money do you need to win a city council or state rep race? Every year new people enter the political process at the "bottom" of the food chain by rounding up their friends and knocking on every single door in the district – twice. There is no more effective tool in American politics than going to the voters and asking for their help. No media tool comes close in comparison. Sure money helps in bigger races but who's to say independents cannot raise more money than Republicans or Democrats? It's just that independent voters have yet to develop an infrastructure to gather and spend those dollars. The money is there waiting to be tapped.

"Oh, now I see. So this is where we start a third political party – to get the money, right?" WRONG – again and always. Building a political party to help independent candidates is the equivalent to rebuilding the post office to deliver music CD's by mail instead of transmitting music via the internet. The day is LONG gone where we need political parties to communicate, organize or raise funds for quality candidates. There are much better ways to get the job done.

But people pick party candidates because parties can be counted on to stand for a platform of consistent positions on key issues, right? Sadly, this one is a common misconception as well. Maybe you could count on parties standing resolute for something in a bygone era but things certainly have changed in the past twenty years. At the national conventions, political parties still go through the motions of building a platform through a committee process. Truth be told this is an exercise in futility. The candidates and incumbents are not bound to support their party platform. There is no enforcement agency to make them vote in accord with their party. The examples of this inconsistency are too myriad to mention but for one that stands out the best. Back in 1996 conservatives were all worked up over the Bob Dole campaign. They worked hard to secure a party platform at the Republican convention that would hold the mercurial Senator from Kansas in line with conservative ideas. There were huge back room wars among big name conservatives as to who was "at the table" in the Dole campaign to secure the candidate to the platform. Within hours of the convention, Dole was on national television telling reporters he had no intention of holding to the party platform. The situation is no better today.

Finally there is the misconception that if everyone in office is not a Democrat or Republican our legislative process will deteriorate into a mess like what they have in Europe. Congress will become like Parliament or the Knesset and nothing will ever get done. Funny how Great Britain and Israel, America's greatest allies keep on moving on in life in spite of this uniquely American opinion.

Furthermore the American Congress already has several members in the House and Senate who are not aligned with the Democrats or Republicans. Those members chose to represent the voters back home instead of the Washington elites. They caucus with whichever party they choose or no party if they choose. They may or may not get more powerful committee assignments but their votes count just as much as any other member's vote when the time for voting arrives.

But what if there is a large bloc of non-aligned members of the House or Senate? Won't they paralyze the current process? Let's think about that a moment. The current process involves two parties in a constant knife fight to destroy each other. The party with the majority completely shuts out the minority. They have no power, no committee chairs, often no opportunity to see legislation until it is time to vote, no time to amend legislation, and in the end almost no one from either party reads the bills they pass. These people hate each other and have paralyzed any honest hope of government for the common good.

So if a large bloc of non-aligned members showed up on Capitol Hill, their votes could determine the leadership, rules of operation, and reconstruct the culture of the Congress. The two existing parties would have to adapt or go home. They could get nothing done – unless they dealt with the concerns of the independent members who place principle over party. Party bosses would have to find common ground again or settle for nothing. For a while this would be both uncomfortable and entertaining. It certainly could not be any more painful than watching the Democrats and Republicans pass trillions of dollars in bailouts and stimulus money without even bothering to read the legislation. What's the worst that could happen?

For too long, people unwittingly married to the status quo have kept Americans locked into the current models. Their biggest tool has been the fear of change. The best answer to these fears is to look back to history. In the founding era people went to Congress to serve not to be served. They placed principle over party and regional interests. They fought hard but worked for common ground for the common good. They did not solve every problem. Many problems they left to the states and local communities. The system was not perfect – but it worked much, much better than it does today.

Our modern inflation of the importance of Washington, D.C. has really twisted the institution of the Congress. Since government has gone on TV we have a lot bigger circus in Washington, D.C. Today members act as if their daily jobs are scripted by soap opera producers. Party leaders stage hearings and media events and play the public like a cheap audience. Media consultants look for candidates like a central casting agency. Every time a major news story hits the airwaves, a casting call goes out across the halls of Congress and members appear on the nightly news to tell us how much they care and how Washington is going to fix this problem for us.

There are some problems Congress is better off not fixing. There will be moments of gridlock and frustration. The system was designed that way because the founders did not believe Congress and the federal government was the final fixer of all problems. They believed Congress and federal law was the last stop, the last resort for fixing problems. Their goal was a balanced system where local governments and state governments took up most of the responsibilities and the federal system played a very specific and limited role. They didn't have TV and 24-hour news cycles back then. So they didn't care how their every action looked to "the American people." What they cared about was the people who elected them and the general health of a constitutional republic. They functioned like people who had to go home every year and live under the laws they passed.

Look back to America just two generations ago. The two political parties were actually functioning as multiple parties in Congress. Democrats and Republicans worked together on the left and the right of many issues. There were conservative Democrats who voted that way – always. There were liberal Republicans who voted left – always. In essence Congress functioned with four political parties and America got along pretty darn well. There were few lockstep, log-rolling leadership power plays that defied common sense and common decency. Placing principle over party and honoring the Constitution above all has worked before in America. It can work again if "We the People" find the courage to make it happen.

So let's review: the reasons we have to keep running the American political process according to the dictates of two political parties is…?

Now that we have most of the common misconceptions out of the way, let's get on to a better model for civil governance.

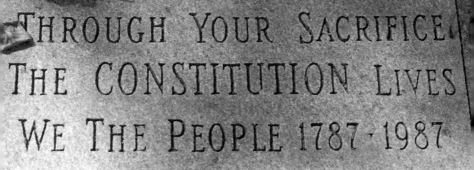

THROUGH YOUR SACRIFICE
THE CONSTITUTION LIVES
WE THE PEOPLE 1787·1987

THE INDEPENDENCE AND LIBERTY
YOU POSSESS ARE THE WORK OF
JOINT COUNCILS AND JOINT
EFFORTS·OF COMMON DANGERS,
SUFFERINGS AND SUCCESS.

WASHINGTON'S FAREWELL ADDRESS SEPT. 17, 1796

Chapter 7:
Free Agents

Yes, the answer really is this simple. The pathway out of the current bondage is for every American to become a free agent again. We know everyone won't take this advice. The good news is there is a critical tipping point on the horizon. If independent Americans get a hold of the real potential in living as free political agents everything can change.

If we could wave a magic wand and simply make political parties disappear what would be lost? Truth is – not much. We are not suggesting passing any law to eliminate parties. That would be foolish and unconstitutional. People have the right to association and if they want to form political parties they are entitled to do so. People have the right to create bowling leagues, bridge clubs and roller coaster riding associations as well. Nobody is talking about banning political parties. What we are talking about is people stepping away from the mentality of bondage and becoming free agents.

A free agent is: <u>A voter who understands the value of their personal franchise.</u>

They realize the Declaration of Independence and the Constitution were written to protect the rights of real individual people not partisan cogs in a party wheel. They refuse to be bound by the party matrix. They seek to find, encourage and empower people to run for political office who stand for principle over party – always. They don't care if a person is a Republican, Democrat, Independent or Martian. They vote for the individual based on a track record of performance not because that person gives a political party more power. Free agents might vote in a Democrat primary one year or a Republican primary next year or cast no primary vote at all. They will back existing candidates or field new candidates in either party or no party. When the parties provide no real leadership, the free agents will find new leaders and help them run and win – including running independent candidates.

What voters are looking for is not a pretty T-shirt or a trip to a boring, taxpayer funded political convention every four years. Real people, paying real taxes and struggling to make a living and support a family want one thing from the political process. They want honest leadership. They want people whose "yes" will be "yes" and whose "no" will be "no."

We don't need political parties to find honest leaders. We don't need monster money to fund campaigns to get honest leaders elected. We don't need high-powered media consultants and huge media buys to manipulate voters with pathetically mundane radio and TV spots.

What we need is for all the people who claim they are sick and tired of the soap opera in the state capitols and Washington, D.C. to start running for office and/or find people who will run and financially support them.

We don't need to establish a political party to do this. We don't need the bureaucracy, overhead, and distractions of such an association. No one can change the country all by himself or herself, so we do need each other but we do not need any of the trappings or bondage of the "partisan spirit" that Washington and Adams warned us avoid. We just need to learn the exact work that has to be done and work together effectively to get it done.

Here is a key to remember – the political parties all rose to power in a non-digital age. They made the most of manipulating the TV generation to take their candidates and their "brands" to prime time but times have changed – a lot. The digital world has now placed both information and the tools of communication in every single living room, kitchen, automobile, church, school and work place in America. This technological revolution has not yet hit the political world in full force – until now.

Still think this is impossible? Let's run some very basic numbers. No one is saying this will be easy but it is not complicated. It is no harder than putting together a good tea party rally or town hall meeting. The difference is, to succeed, you have to stick with the plan for a period of years. This is where the establishment politicians are counting on you to fail. They don't think "the American people" have the intelligence and courage to stick with a plan to displace the ruling class. They figure they will outlast you because they get paid to run the country and you don't. Even worse, they get paid from your paycheck before you even get your paycheck so they figure you are the slave and they are the masters. Of course they don't talk that way out loud in front of the cameras – but behind the scenes when no one is recording, I have heard them talking about you. They don't believe you have the stuff to take your country back from them. They simply plan to outlast your outrage and temper tantrums and then tighten the chains so you have to behave better in the future.

Do they hate you? Of course they do not. The opposite of love is not hate, it is indifference. One of the great curses of a "public life" is politicians lose the ability to see people as people. They begin to divide the world between them and the rest of us. Sure we are all people, but some people are just more special than others and politicians are the special people. Everything in the culture of the statehouse and on Capitol Hill reinforces they are special. That's why, when you hear a politician talking about "the American people" you know they have been drinking the Kool-Aid. They are no longer in office to help their neighbors and friends in the district back home where they live too. They are telling us with their words that they have transferred their identity to the ruling class. They have divided the world between them and the rest of us.

Breaking this model of division and bondage will not be easy, but the plan is simple. The math does not exceed the eighth grade level. It does not take 40 hours per week to accomplish. It does take faith, perseverance and a restructuring of priorities. So the body politic, the Independents, Tea Party people and everyone who watches all those cable shows and listens to talk radio will have to make some decisions and spend some time on task. If we do this together – America will change for the better.

Here is an honest plan, worked out over 30 years of applied political experience. There is nothing new in this plan. It was the same process that won Abraham Lincoln the presidency in 1860. It worked in the 1960's and as long as we keep working it, the plan will keep creating the good results. It begins with a little math but don't worry; this is not a story problem.

The mathematics of real change:

- In the average Congressional district there are roughly 600,000 people.
- On average about 300,000 TOTAL votes are cast in a general election race for the U.S. Congress.
- So it takes one more vote than 50% of the votes cast to win. Thus a Congressional race can be won with 150,001 votes (theoretically of course).
- A landslide victory of 60% to 40% would give the winner 180,000 votes and the loser 120,000 votes. That's a winning margin of 60,000 votes.
- So if you are in a district that is so lopsided that the incumbent always wins you are probably looking at needing to turn around 60,000 votes in your district – worst-case scenario. There are plenty of U.S. House districts where the threshold for victory is much lower. We will stick with this worst-case scenario for most of this example just so no one can accuse us of underestimating the difficulty of this challenge.

Wait a minute. Changing 60,000 votes is impossible because the incumbents of both parties have so much money that they control everything all the time so what's the use?

The above run-on sentence is the single biggest real reason America is in the mess we are in today. Most people just give up before they even try. The political establishment has so weighted the rules, collected the money, and rigged the system that they just know people won't fight to win their Congress back. It's jut too hard. They expect you to buy another bag of potato chips, rent another video, and just stay home and ignore the problem for another election. It's just like being in a schoolyard dominated by a gang of bullies. They plan on intimidating you every single day until you hand over your lunch money and sit in the corner and cry.

Are you tired of being bullied? Then here is a news flash for you. All that money they banter around to intimidate you… it's all designed to be spent in an election model from the 1980's. Do they plan on going door-to-door, meeting-to-meeting, community-by-community? Heck NO! They are incumbent members of Congress for goodness sake. They don't walk neighborhoods and visit the peasants back home. When is the last time you saw your member of Congress – other than on a TV commercial? Most people can't even tell you the name of their U.S. Representative unless you give them a big clue. That is exactly the way political consultants want it. They want to spend a ton of money in the last two weeks to remind you to go out and vote for the incumbent who is a great American, loves puppies and children, and always votes for world peace. They have been doing it this way for 30 years and are not about to change now. They don't disclose the fact that the consultants make a sweet 15% commission on the placement of all those ads, plus their monthly consulting fees. So why would they want to suddenly have to design and run a real grassroots campaign that is genuinely hard work?

The whole campaign sweetheart system is set up for radio and TV buys. That presumes of course that NO ONE is in the district every day registering voters, organizing voters and training up new leadership. The incumbents don't do ANY of these things we are talking about and have no intention of doing so. Nor can they do so because they are tied to the elitist culture of Washington. You, on the other hand, have all year, 24/7 to build an army in the district and forward new leadership. They have money – yes – but their money is only designed to be spent in the final thirty days of the election. By that time, you will have built a network of real people who vote. Your people networks won't need a TV commercial to tell them what to do on Election Day. They will have already made that decision for themselves.

How do you find those 60,000 votes?

First start with a network of leaders in the community. Who do you know that works with a network of people? The network can be 10 people in a bowling league, a church of one hundred people, a small corporation or a person with a great Christmas card list. Everyone has a network of people, especially in the internet age.

Start by meeting together. Pull your network together and give them a copy of this book. Get them hooked up online and the journey has begun.

Step 1: is to give everyone a copy of the Declaration of Independence and Constitution. Anyone unwilling to read those two core documents you don't have to worry about working with. You will find a number of important resources at the back of this book that will also lend some help.

How often do you need to meet? As often as necessary and as little as possible. In this world of digital communications what is important is the transfer of information – NOT gathering bodies in a single room or amphitheater. Big meetings are fine and fun for a while; but the important work is done very simply, household-to-household through the transfer of information and encouragement.

Step 2: <u>Learn and teach the process of voter registration in your state.</u> This can be as simple as downloading a single page from the Secretary of State's office. Every state has their own rules but none of them are burdensome. Get the forms, learn the rules and then begin to set goals. Everyone in your network becomes a voter registration advocate. Everyone makes sure their network is 100% registered to vote.

Step 3: <u>Find a candidate or several candidates you can support.</u> Now here is the real key in the process. The model is based on running someone for the U.S. House of Representatives. That is a much bigger model than running someone for city council, municipal mayor or state representative. We have intentionally defaulted to the hard side of the equation. By doing so we are forcing ourselves to train for a marathon when a lot of races can be run in much shorter time with less effort. That's OK. We are focusing on the toughest Congressional race in the worst-case scenario because your team will be like the Navy Seals. You will have trained in a model so hard that winning will become a habit.

Sometimes you won't have to find a brand new candidate. There are some people out there in public office that are worth supporting. Some are worth promoting to higher office. Some need to leave their current office and should run for another position. It doesn't matter what their political party affiliation

is – if they vote the right way consistently and fit the profile of support for the Declaration and Constitution you can turn your network to support them as well.

Let's talk about the candidates for a moment. Here is a good formula for vetting candidates.

- **First Question:** Are they willing to support and defend the Declaration of Independence, the Constitution and the principles upon which those documents stand? If they are, then you have a potential candidate.
- **Second Question:** What is their track record? Where is the evidence that they will live out the answer to the first question? How do they live and conduct daily business? What offices have they held and what is their track record? Does the walk match the talk?
- **Third Question:** Is this person willing to work as hard as necessary to win this race and willing to run two or three times if necessary to win this seat?

Here is where things always get a little sticky. Very few of your allies and networks will have exactly the same priorities on what they want most in a candidate. This is where we have to go back to first principles and hold the line of leadership. The basic operational platform for American civil government is the Declaration of Independence and the Constitution. If candidates don't hold to those documents, then why bother supporting them? If they do hold to those documents, then we are going to be arguing about priorities. Here is where most movements split apart and fail – the leaders get the cart in front of the horse.

Take a deep breath. Look away from this book for a moment and refocus your eyes on something far away and then come back.

Now, here is a critical principle of leadership in a constitutional, representative republic: <u>If you are looking for the perfect candidate or nothing – you will get nothing every time.</u>

The battle for liberty under law is won or lost in the struggle for ground gained by inches and yards over a generation. On the rarest of occasions there is a stunning victory where a great amount of ground is taken in a single day. It does not happen very often. This is not a high school student council we are talking about. This is the grandest form of civil government created and sustained in human history. You don't just shake it like a dog's chew toy every two years. <u>The goal of good government, based on the Declaration and the Constitution, is a lifetime endeavor. So we seek to keep moving ever forward toward the goal, which means: you don't have to find a perfect candidate. They need to be the</u>

<u>best person you can find in that moment of time.</u>

You are not electing them to be a king or queen for life. You are asking them to serve according to core principles for a period of time and come home. If they don't come home or run for another office after eight years – then find another candidate to run against them. You are free agents. You can support anyone you like, whenever you like. No party owns you.

Candidate selection is where the best movements break apart. People have deep-seated convictions about different issues. The right to life, liberty and property are fundamental to the Declaration and Constitution. In this modern era, however, many people have priorities that clash. Some will only support a pro-life candidate. Some define pro-life more broadly than others. Some want a balanced budget NOW, not two or four years from now. Some think the right to bear arms is the most important issue, others claim it is national defense.

This is where common sense must prevail. There are no perfect candidates because there are no perfect people. If you look in the mirror and consider yourself the perfect candidate – please give this book to someone else. This plan is NOT for you

Since there are no perfect candidates your team has to put the best person on the field and back them. If you cannot find a person who meets your threshold of constitutional principles then move on to another race. We can't fix this mess in one season. This will take a while.

You are not marrying any candidates. You are not pasting your soul upon them. They are not your Saviour or knight in shining armor. A candidate is your neighbor sent to do a limited task of public service for a limited amount of time. Find the one who best fits the profile of supporting the principles of the Declaration and Constitution and support them for office. Get behind them, give them money and then hold them accountable once elected. Don't campaign for them as a messiah. Just tell people you are backing them because they are the best person you could find for this race in this hour.

The Irish-born Member of Parliament, Edmund Burke is often quoted as saying, "All that is required for evil to triumph is for good men to do nothing." If they were good men in the first place, then how could they do nothing? Good men most certainly must care about overcoming evil, or how could Burke consider them good at all. Perhaps Burke understood the greatest challenge for good people is to overcome the paralysis and division of "the perfect or nothing" syndrome. If you keep your eye on the big picture – a civil government where elected officials abide by the Declaration, the Constitution and the principles on which they stand it will get easier. Especially if you constantly remember that this kind of reform will take time. There will be many elections, many candidates, many opportunities for constant improvement. You don't have to win everything today or do nothing.

If you get really stuck here try reading David McCullogh's classic work, *John Adams*. You might also consider the HBO series by the same name on DVD. In that work you can see the life of one of America's greatest patriots and certainly one the greatest mind's of the founding era. Adams was constantly challenged by people who did not "get it." He endured the endlessly distracted Benjamin Franklin for a lifetime. He did mental battle with the misguided affections of Thomas Jefferson to the end of their days. Adams did not give up or walk away when he failed to get all he hoped for. He was frustrated, angry and depressed (often) but he kept on plodding toward the goal. The perfect or nothing would have left Adams on the side of the road of discontent. He kept struggling toward the ideals of liberty under law. In the end, Dr. Benjamin Rush paid Adams one of the greatest compliments of his life. He told his old friend, in the midst of all the chaos and confusion of the founding era, "You thought for us John." It was Adams ideas that prevailed because he never surrendered to the frustration of the imperfect moment.

Step 4: <u>Turn on the numbers machine.</u>

Please remember this is a Navy Seal training model. We are assuming the worst-case scenario: that you must find a candidate to support against a "landslide" incumbent member of Congress. It won't always be this difficult but let's stick with the challenge.

The election is in November, so we must register 60,000 voters before the registration deadline in your state. Now we take the core allies we have assembled and turn on the "viral" voter registration effort. Everybody registers everybody they can find. Wherever you run across people who are with you but are already registered you do two things:

A) You thank them and ask them to give you a contact address (snail mail and email) so you can send them free, helpful information before the election.

B) You hand them two voter registration forms and ask them if they will hand them out to people who are not registered but who care.

C) CAREFULLY add every new name and address (from step A) into a computer database. Do this progressively so you don't end up with a box of forms that will take hours to input data. This information is gold so treat it very carefully.

The goal here is to build an army of registered voters large enough to charge the hill on Election Day and win. It would be really cool to do that with 60,000 brand new or re-registered voters but that seldom happens. Somewhere along the way you will build a database that exceeds 60,000 voters new and currently registered. Don't stop; build the biggest list you possibly can.

Step 5: <u>Get organized and take-up a collection.</u>

Don't you love it? We got all this way without having to be all that organized or expensive. Now we have to raise some money so we can stay in touch with the army of good people that has been assembled. How much money? Here is the great news. The traditional candidates will be spending millions to reach people on radio and TV. In a big media market the very best afternoon drive radio show might reach 30,000 people with an ad buy. You already have a database, that is hand-built and fully qualified, that is twice that size!

So let's try to raise all the money we can. Hire a few needy college students to make phone call follow-ups with the people who recently registered either to vote or with you. Start calling them just to say thank you. Where you don't have phone numbers send pre-printed post cards and send emails.

Step 6: <u>Let the fun begin!</u>

Congratulations, now that you have done the tough stuff – throw a party! Invite all your leaders, friends, network associates, every person on your list, everyone from your church, school and everyone you possibly can to a tea-party, town-hall, Celebration of Liberty! The purpose of this meeting is to introduce all your new friends to each other and to explain just how this new model for leadership is working. This is your chance to teach more of the basics on voter registration and communications. And it is an excellent opportunity to introduce the people running for public office in your area, especially the ones you are most excited about. It is always a good idea to invite all the people running for a specific office but that is something for your team to figure out.

Here's one more important suggestion that is hard to follow. Once you have gotten this far, if egos have not taken over, beware. Very few people can gather a crowd without someone just dying to get to the microphone. It will happen, it always does, so get ready. There are few things you can do to mitigate against the inevitable.

- Keep your leadership network very small. Don't hand anybody a title in return for their help. Send those people to work for the political parties.

• Do not play with the media. You don't need them, they need you. Advertising and PR are NOT critical at this stage of the game. Remember you are NOT building a political party. You are an assembly of free agents. You gather together for a single purpose: raising up principled leadership in your area.

• Do NOT call the media and ask them to cover your big meeting. You might only get half the people you expected. Who cares? The meeting is not to prove anything to the public. You already are building the army. The meeting is to encourage the troops and help them meet the candidates you are considering for support.

My, my, my, won't the political establishment be surprised. Without a news conference or bevy of celebrity superstars, without a multi-million dollar budget you and your pals built a network of concerned citizens who are now ready to provide principle-based leadership to America. That's the way Sam Adams did it. That's the way Abe Lincoln did it. That's the way you can do it too.

Step 7: <u>Rinse and repeat all the way to Election Day.</u>
This formula works better the more you work it. Some of your hopefuls will lose their races. That's OK. There is always another election coming. The key is to start with quality people and support them so they can keep running until

people know them and trust them enough to give them a chance to get elected.

But wait a minute – there has to be a lot more communicating, right? What about Election Day, yard signs, etc.? You will be amazed how smart people become on all those matters. As individuals they will find amazing and creative ways to network and promote the people they want to support. From this point you'll quickly figure out the rest. The less organization the better in this regard. Encourage people to act as individuals, not as "members" of anything. As individuals they have lots of opportunities to get involved without running into state and federal election law barriers. All of this activity is legal, it is just a matter of getting it to fit into the right legal boxes. Individuals have the most leeway. They can give money to campaigns or to a PAC that can legally forward the funds to a campaign. You can help people find those networks or build your own PAC or work with an existing PAC. (More details in chapter 8)

Additional Strategic Options

Losing to Win

Sometimes people will all agree to back a candidate in a race that cannot be won. That strategy is legitimate. Running a great campaign and losing is still a move forward if the candidate understands he or she will be right back at it the day after the election and running again in two years. The effort was not wasted.

The Blocking Strategy

There will also be times you might decide to take on both parties and run an independent candidate. Your candidate may not win. He/She may actually cause a Republican or Democrat challenger to lose. Or your "blocking" effort may tumble a popular incumbent and let a worse candidate get elected. This is the scenario the Republicans get all worked up about. Those who still believe their party is the "conservative" party are terrified that independent actions will wipe out the Republican party. If they really believed that, then why are they not doing more to put forward candidates independents can vote for? You see there are two sides to that argument.

The blocking strategy is a good one because it presents political parties with real accountability. They cannot control the whole field so they must come to terms with real voters who will not be intimidated. You may block a mediocre candidate and get a worse one for two years. The republic will survive for two years. Your goal has to be to run and win a better candidate the very next election. This is a strategic loss to win a better position in 24 months. The strategy works if you faithfully stick with it.

The Not on Top Campaign

There will be times you get stuck. You may not be able to find a candidate for the General Election. Things go wrong now and then. So what if you are stuck with two bad choices. Guess what? You can skip that race and encourage everyone you know to do the same. Lots of big-ticket races are won by 100,000 votes or less. Jimmy Carter won the Presidency in Ohio in 1976 by about one vote per precinct. We all know what 537 votes in Florida did to the Presidential election in 2000. So a network of free agents can be effective at many levels, even in the races at the top of the ticket. If they have to take a walk, then enjoy the view. The key is to stay at this with a better candidate next time.

Now for really good news: IT WON'T ALWAYS BE THIS HARD!

If you execute this plan faithfully, if you seek to build an army capable of conquering a "landslide" congressional district, you and your Navy Seals will find a myriad of opportunities to support state reps, city council members, mayors and school board members. As you recruit, train and empower those new leaders they will be building network affinity and trust with voters so that they will be excellent candidates to run for Congress some day soon. When they do – they will be bringing a big part of the landslide with them!

Consider this example. The free agent model is set up for the worst-case scenario. But what if the race for Congress is truly competitive? In 2008 the 8th Congressional District in Orlando, Florida was won by a margin of ONLY 52% to 48%. The margin of victory was 13,364 votes. Divide that by two and you get 6682 votes. That's a lot less than 60,000 votes, right? Change 6683 votes in that district and the opponent wins the race.

Nobody said this would be easy – but we did say it would be simple. Not quite as simple as throwing tea into Boston Harbor but remember the colonists did not become a nation just because of a protest movement. That first tea party really ticked off the Parliament but what really hurt was when the colonists started drinking coffee instead of tea. That change of lifestyle sent economic shock waves into the British economy. The story of colonial sacrifices grew into a long, bitter War for Independence. To displace the tyranny of the elitist ruling class in America today there will be sacrifices. We will all have to get off the couch. We will have to read books again, get out into our communities, knock on some doors, and give some real time and money. None of this is rocket science. It's just hard, honest work.

A final note on this plan: you will notice that nowhere along the line did we suggest that you build an empire and run for political office yourself. You might feel called to run someday and you might succeed. If you do, please don't ever forget where you came from and the principles upon which this nation stands. Remember, you must come home someday and face your neighbors. If you do lose your way, they will be adding your name to the list of people who need to be retired on the next Election Day.

130

Chapter 8:
Time for Questions

As we have presented this plan over the years a number of the same questions always arise, such as:

Where have these ideas and this plan actually worked?

As stated before, this plan is not original. The idea of working from the bottom-up and building a base of voter support is nothing new. Over the years we have known several politicians who have built this kind of model and been elected and re-elected for a long time. There are members in Congress today who have followed this formula. When a politician gets elected from the bottom-up, there is not a whole lot the parties in power can do to pressure him/her to vote according to anyone's dictates. If they threaten the member with a primary challenge – who cares? When you elect people with a strong base of citizen support back home they are able to stand strong against the establishment insiders.

What do we call ourselves? We are not a political party but we are an organized network so what do we tell people?

Tell them you are free agents, plain and simple. You are citizens exercising your God-given rights to free speech and association. You are free agents working together for honest leadership. A number of us have gravitated to the website and tag line of iVoters.com. The "i" obviously stands for independent. If you like bumper stickers or window decals, iVoters.com has a few really cool ones available.

But don't we have to have a platform?

Sure, we've got one. It's the Declaration and Constitution and the principles upon which they stand. If you need more see the Democrats and Republicans. They have been outside the national boundary lines for so many years that they will be happy to sign up a new member.

Why are we starting with Congress?

This strategy works on concepts such as critical mass and tipping points. Starting with a statewide race or the race for the Presidency is a bit too large a target to leverage from the start. More importantly, there is way too much emphasis on the White House. The Executive Branch is cool and a bit like the Superbowl but it is also just as anticlimactic. The lawmaking branch of the government is the Congress. If the Congress is doing the right thing in right proportions, the

White House has to go along. That's the way the system was set up to work. Not a President dictating his will to the nation and Congress cowering in the corner afraid of the President's popularity. That has never worked regardless of who is in the White House. The Congress is the vehicle designed for the expression of the will of the people. It is our duty to embrace that opportunity and get it right.

There are 435 members of the House and 100 members of the Senate. If free agents change the make up of just 10% of the House (44 members) the whole dynamic of the Congress changes. That's less than one race per state. If free agents change just 100 seats... do the math. This strategy works if "We the People" work at it.

If free agents change just two House seats in a battleground state, the leverage of their networks can multiply to make a critical difference in a U.S. Senate race. Yes, this will take time and real diligence – but real change is far from impossible.

The Republicans and their talk show allies say you are going to split their party and destroy America.
Yawn.
Do they really think we are all that stupid? America needs a lot of help and a lot of new leaders. If the Republicans or Democrats want to forward candidates who are willing to

keep the oath of office they take (to support and defend the Constitution) people will certainly consider them. In the end it's all about good people. If they have them, lets see them. They have to compete for our votes now. Maybe they are just whining because we are raising the standards.

The Republicans are all about free markets, competition and choice. So why don't they want to compete for real voters in the real world? If competition makes us better in business and education then won't it make us better in the realm of leadership and civil government?

Do we have to register as a PAC (political action committee) to do this?

There are two issues here: state law and federal law. Lets start with the feds. You are on safe legal ground to do the basic voter registration and citizenship training without owing the government any paperwork. In spite of the onerous campaign laws (passed by Democrats and Republicans to intimidate and silence you) the courts are still fighting to keep free speech alive in America. So from a federal perspective you are on pretty safe ground so far.

Once you decide to give money or support a specific candidate for federal office then the federal laws kick in. If you are giving as an individual then there are contribution limits. You give the check and the candidate files the paperwork. If you want to get everybody together to give to a central fund then you have to file papers with the Federal Election Commission to become a PAC. It's not complicated to file, but you have to do some reading to learn how to abide by the regulations. One way to get around the hassle is to link up with an existing PAC that is willing to help you. The Liberty Committee is a national PAC willing to work with free agent networks around the country. You can be a part of that PAC and follow their established guidelines to multiply your influence (www. libertycommittee.com).

Every state has their own rules on political contributions and here the world can get a little weird. State lawmakers have been secretly hostile to citizen movements for a generation. They have been passing unconstitutional laws anticipating you might finally show up and start sending them back home to get real jobs. So in some states, like Florida, they have tried to set up a bunch of ridiculous hoops. The courts have been doing a serious smack-down on these laws in recent years so don't be afraid.

Start now by going online and reading through your state election laws. It will take a few hours and you will have some questions. Talk around your networks. Call the Secretary of State's office and ask for help on questions you may not understand. For more help contact iVoters.com. This website offers a lot of help on getting you over the hump in your state. Remember, the laws were put there as barriers to intimidate you. The people who wrote the laws, live by them everyday inside their political party fiefdoms. They have to obey the same laws you do, which is a real switch. So if they can do it – you can to. The key is to find out where the hoops are and follow proper regulations. It's not that tough.

They cannot stop you from talking and getting together and helping people get registered to vote. They cannot stop you from encouraging people to learn the Declaration and the Constitution and to enter public service. Nobody can legally do that.

Going to tea parties was lots of fun. Yelling loud at the town hall meetings was even better, especially when the media showed up. Can't we just stick to this stuff? Why do we have to get all focused and organized and give money? Are you sure you are not a plant from the Republican Party? Sorry, for answering that question with a question but this is exactly what the major parties are hoping for. They believe the tea party movement and independent voters in general are just a passing fad. In two years they will all fade away and only the paid party professionals will be left. They are banking their whole careers that you will never grow up and take responsibility for your political representation.

This plan is the same thing groups like the NRA, and ACORN do, isn't it?
You might want to throw multi-level marketers and church groups in there as well. Getting people organized for a common goal is not exactly an original idea. People have been doing this a long time. The difference is the NRA and single-issue organizations only gather people to focus on THEIR issue and use their numbers as a wedge against the system. By becoming so tightly focused they radically reduce their impact. Furthermore, single-issue groups almost always make the same mistake by committing their agenda to a single political party. The NRA is not very welcome in national Democrat circles. The Sierra Club does not host Republican events. By driving their single issue into a single party these groups cut their potential influence in half.

Free agents are doing exactly the opposite. We are calling the entire nation and the political process back to the founding principles of the Declaration and the Constitution. We will work with anyone, Independent, Democrat, Republican or Martian that stands for these core realities This wide focus benefits the entire nation because the government works best when principles rise over partisanship.

Maybe you haven't heard of George Soros? Don't you know how powerful his empire has become in America?

Yep, we saw George Soros and the shadow party coming a long way down the road. We knew Arianna Huffington when she claimed she was a conservative and disagreed with her back then as we do now.

What Soros and company have done is to hollow out the core of the Democrat party and refill it with organizations made over in his radical philosophy. Soros and his allies represent a fractional percentage of the American population. Soros, Peter Lewis (founder of Progressive Insurance) and a few of their radical allies have focused hundreds of millions of dollars on the American political process. They have underwritten PAC's that recruit radical candidates. They have networked with the most radical elements and funneled all their energies into taking over Congress from the left. Since only a fraction of America understands or agrees with the Soros agenda their empire sits upon a very narrow base of support. That's why they are in such a hurry. Their money will only take them so far. Since their ideas don't work they can only fleece the public with rhetoric and guilt for so long. Once people get the whole truth about these people and their agenda they will be run out of town.

So why not just sit back and wait for the radical left to fail?

There are a few reasons that won't work. First they could genuinely bankrupt America in the process. Soros almost destroyed the economy of Great Britain at one point in his career. He was convicted for illegal dealings in France. He does not exactly play according to the standard rules of right and wrong. Secondly, 20 years ago Soros could not get to power because the WWII generation was still around and not about to buy into this radical nonsense. That generation is largely gone today. In their place is a group of young people, raised in public education where they have barely seen the Constitution or the Declaration, let alone studied them or sacrificed to defend them. Soros and company know America is much weaker today than it was thirty years ago. They are seeking to pick the bones of a nation that has lost its core identity. Finally, if we permit these people to control Congress and rewrite America, a lot of people will get hurt badly in the process. History proves that totalitarian elitists don't take well to opposition. Look at the end of the 20th century and see how the Soros model deals with basic human rights.

But Soros has a weakness – a fatal flaw. There are over 300 million people in America. Most of them don't know who he is. He has never run for public office or been in the general public. He is the CEO of the Shadow Party and unquestionably operating off a private, personal agenda. He buys his friends and allies. Sure, he is a multi-billionaire but on Election Day he can only cast one vote.

You don't have to buy your friends. The agenda of the free agents in America is transparent. It is the Declaration, the Constitution and the principles upon which they stand. We didn't invent this stuff and we are not trying to take over anything. We are simply standing on the shoulders of those true Americans who have paid the price for all of our liberty, across all races, creeds, colors, religions and economic strata. We are standing mid-stream in the mainstream of American identity. People like Soros come and go – the self-evident truths remain.

Are you *sure* you are not trying to start a third party?
The definition of insanity is … starting a third political party when the first two don't belong here in the first place and are totally irrelevant. Why start and build a bureaucratic infrastructure that will suck up money, time, encourage massive egos and corruption – when that is exactly what we are trying to stop. Can we be any more clear on this one?

But if we do this free agent plan really well, what happens if the Democrats and Republicans put forth candidates

that both have a clear record of honoring the Declaration and Constitution? What do you do then?

Run an independent who agrees to the same and declare victory. Then start teaching others how to do exactly the same things you just accomplished.

Chapter 9:
What Does Victory
Look Like?

This effort was not started in Washington, D.C. by design.

The message of free agency is not fronted by mega-personalities from the Hollywood Hills. This work is being built from the bottom-up, community by community, with real everyday people who do most of the working and paying in this country. There is no attempt to "get the media to cover this story" or place this effort on the big news programs, or on Oprah. This is about changing the way we think, the way we live, and the way we conduct ourselves in relational integrity. This is transparent and intentional.

There are many who scoff at this work and declare it a lost cause. Even though there are undeniable signs that real change is coming, many of political big wigs consider this whole idea of free agency a lost cause. They believe machine politics, in a "two-party dress" is the inevitable reality of American life. For them it is has always been this way and it will always be so. Funny, they used to say the same thing about the Soviet politburo.

What does victory look like?

This task of American renewal will take a while. It will not be finished in an election or two. We'll know we have crossed the finish line when:

- We stop worshipping celebrities and start thinking for ourselves.
- The family once again becomes the first school for teaching the truth.
- The majority of people view themselves as free agents, freeing their minds so they can support real leaders regardless of political parties.
- The consensus of the culture is to return to the first principles of the Declaration of Independence and the Constitution as currently amended.
- We accept the daily duty to hold all branches of government accountable to those core documents and principles.

- We are more concerned about raising up quality leaders than athletic and entertainment superstars and we spend our money to support those leaders.
- The people running for public office know they must win the trust of the voters once again, instead of cutting deals with party kingpins.
- "We the People" care more about a Congress that honors the Constitution than we do about who sits in the White House.
- We elect people based on the content of their character and track record not because of any party affiliation. And we put our money where our mouth is.
- The American government functions under the same rules and realities as the people who pay the bills for that government.

When Jeff Smith (Jimmy Stewart) went to Washington to serve in the U.S. Senate he became every man in America. Frank Capra's Oscar-winning story, "Mr. Smith Goes to Washington," produced in 1939, is as relevant as today's Internet news headlines. Jeff Smith was an idealist. He believed the words of the founders. He went to Washington to serve his country and his constituents. When he got there he was told such patriotism was a lost cause. He was told to check his principles and his hat at the front door. The town and the Congress were both run by the party machine.

Senator Smith could not force his view of America into that matrix and got himself into a front-page showdown with the party machine.

In his closing filibuster speech, Jeff Smith held the Senate and the country spellbound. The political class threw everything at him they could. They mocked him, excluded him and eventually destroyed his reputation through false accusations. He had no chance as one lowly citizen against the machine. On the Senate floor, Mr. Smith's last words to his scoffing critics were about lost causes.

"All you people don't know about lost causes... Lost causes are the only ones worth fighting for. The only reason any man ever fights for them is because of just one plain simple rule: 'Love thy neighbor.' And in this world full of hatred a man who knows that one rule has a great trust. You know that you fight for the lost causes harder than for any other, yes, you even die for them..."

Where is Mr. Smith today? Where are the people willing to sacrifice for first principles, not from rage, or selfish ambition but because 'Love thy neighbor" is not a suggestion, but a sacred duty? Beyond the tea parties, town halls, protest meetings, funny signs and angry threats lies a window of incredible opportunity. This generation has the opportunity to overcome decades of darkness and decline and rekindle the American Spirit. Now is the time to move past the protests, unite as free agents, and get on with the hard work of rebuilding this greatest of all human adventures called America.

Chapter 10: Get Free and Stay Free

This entire book has been careful to try to avoid the worn out political clichés of the era. The struggles America is experiencing are not original to the 21st century. In spite of our desire to pretend we are somewhere no one has ever been before, we are not there. We are here and Americans have been here before. The foundational questions beneath the current arguments over health care, taxation, national defense, energy and the environment are not brand new. So we will conclude with an old cliché that is often repeated today: Enough is enough.

Enough talk. Enough of cable TV and talk radio celebrities telling us what is wrong with America but NEVER telling us how to fix the problems. (Clue to the culture: the media celebrities – left and right – may not know the solution. Fixing the problem is not in their contract, nor a part of their life experience).

Enough of political parties trying to capture the tea party movement or defame, mock and destroy it. Both parties and their high-paid consultants are not happy that any people group would dare awaken from the matrix of the two party system. The concept of "independent thought" is not the goal of Democrats or Republicans.

Enough of activists demanding, "I want my country back." This never was your exclusive country. Your name is not on the Declaration of Independence. We all inherited this gift of Liberty. Let's start working on getting "our" country back in constitutional order by sacrificing our lives, fortunes and sacred honor on her behalf.

Enough of waiting for "the right candidate" to come along and fix everything by running for President. May God deliver America from such a destructive delusion.

Enough of waiting on political parties to lead. If we don't step up and lead with a principled, people-centered plan such as this one, we deserve the bondage in which this Congress is placing us.

Enough of the vertical illusion. The answer will not come from the top-down, not now or ever. The answer is here at the bottom where "We the People" live. All political power in America was designed to flow from "We the People." We don't need superstructures. We need normal people doing super hard work.

Enough words. Enough of this book. This plan is not yet perfect or complete but there is enough here to take a new battle for Independence all the way from your hands and heart to Washington, D.C. and back again. Godspeed.

Independence Hall
The State House of
Pennsylvania

The Birthplace of
the UNITED STATES
of AMERICA

Appendix

What the Tea Parties Need

This book has been written for all Americans, those on the couch and those in the streets. Thus we waited until the appendix to specifically discuss the tea parties so prominent in America at the time of this printing. If those groups are to survive and thrive for years to come then two suggestions might be helpful.

First – the tea parties must move beyond an agenda of protest and become a movement based on content. The homemade signs and zeal can only get you so far. Over a lifetime we have seen movements ebb and flow, come and go and most end up like burnt toast. The fires of political protest and zeal can only be stoked so hot for so long.

We suggest the best content for sustaining a platform of responsible citizenship is found in the Declaration of Independence, the Constitution as it is currently written, and the principles upon which those two documents stand. It is very important that those seeking to lead in America own up to those two defining documents. They are the heartbeat of Liberty.

In addition, it is important to read what the founding generation had to say about these documents, but to do so by reading the actual writings of the founders. We need to understand where they got their ideas. What were they reading? What principles built their worldview? Academics love to spin the founding era to fit their personal agendas so just reading a history text book published in 2000 is NOT going to get you back to the sources. There are modern authors like David McCullough whose commitment to accuracy in history makes his works well worth reading. McCullough's classic on John Adams is one of the best ever written. Even as good as this work is – the founders still have plenty to offer in their original words that you can read without ever leaving your home.

This book is intentionally short to encourage people who have fallen out of the habit of reading or never really liked it much. You cannot rebuild a nation without gaining an understanding of real historical content. That material requires reading books and honest study. There is a list of websites, DVD's, and radio broadcasts to help get you warmed up to the task, but sooner or later to get to solid content you're going to have to crack a book.

The next essential for the tea parties to capture is strategy. Hopefully this basic primer on how to move new leaders forward into civil government will be considered worth serious consideration. There are other ways to go about this, but we only presented the strategy that we are convinced works best and is most essential.

What we are not saying is perhaps even more important. Many believe what the tea parties need the most is a leader to unite them and turn them into a political steamroller. Maybe.

There is one all too predictable pitfall in that leadership paradigm. If the tea parties go "vertical" and build a centralized command-control system, it won't be long before they look like the political parties and the bureaucracy they are currently opposing. The key to the next American revolution is the understanding that "going vertical" in politics is a very dangerous business. The most effective way for the tea parties to make a real difference is to follow the pattern of the founding colonies. They made their politics local. They sent their very best people into their colonial legislatures. They spent most of their time on local government. Only after the War for Independence, did the states create a federal structure to unite them in a very limited constitutional formula.

The way to change America in the 21st century is from the bottom-up. This is where the tea parties began and hopefully where they will keep their primary base of operations. You can elect state lawmakers, members of Congress and even Presidents from where you live right now. Networking across the nation of course makes sense, working together as well, but the best strategy has always been: All politics is local. If you build strong networks at the bottom, taking care of the top is a lot easier.

More Materials to Get Started:

1776, by David McCullough

John Adams, by David McCullough

Sam Adams, by Mark Puls

Defending the Declaration, Gary Amos

Christianity and the Constitution, John Eidsmoe

John Adams, DVD by HBO

Gettysburg , DVD by Turner Home Entertainment

God Won't Vote This Year, by David Zanotti

The Commission, by David Zanotti

The Patriot's Handbook, by Dr. George Grant

The History of the American People, by Paul Johnson

The Public Square® Radio Program, *Archived Broadcasts on Rediscovering American History available online at aproundtable.org*

The Declaration of Independence of the United States of America

IN CONGRESS, July 4, 1776.

The unanimous Declaration of the thirteen united States of America,

When in the Course of human events, it becomes necessary for one people to dissolve the political bands which have connected them with another, and to assume among the powers of the earth, the separate and equal station to which the Laws of Nature and of Nature's God entitle them, a decent respect to the opinions of mankind requires that they should declare the causes which impel them to the separation.

We hold these truths to be self-evident, that all men are

created equal, that they are endowed by their Creator with certain unalienable Rights, that among these are Life, Liberty and the pursuit of Happiness.--That to secure these rights, Governments are instituted among Men, deriving their just powers from the consent of the governed, --That whenever any Form of Government becomes destructive of these ends, it is the Right of the People to alter or to abolish it, and to institute new Government, laying its foundation on such principles and organizing its powers in such form, as to them shall seem most likely to effect their Safety and Happiness. Prudence, indeed, will dictate that Governments long established should not be changed for light and transient causes; and accordingly all experience hath shewn, that mankind are more disposed to suffer, while evils are sufferable, than to right themselves by abolishing the forms to which they are accustomed. But when a long train of abuses and usurpations, pursuing invariably the same Object evinces a design to reduce them under absolute Despotism, it is their right, it is their duty, to throw off such Government, and to provide new Guards for their future security.--Such has been the patient sufferance of these Colonies; and such is now the necessity which constrains them to alter their former Systems of Government. The history of the present King of Great Britain is a history of repeated injuries and usurpations, all having in direct object the establishment of an absolute Tyranny over these States. To prove this, let Facts be submitted to a candid world.

He has refused his Assent to Laws, the most wholesome

and necessary for the public good.

He has forbidden his Governors to pass Laws of immediate and pressing importance, unless suspended in their operation till his Assent should be obtained; and when so suspended, he has utterly neglected to attend to them.

He has refused to pass other Laws for the accommodation of large districts of people, unless those people would relinquish the right of Representation in the Legislature, a right inestimable to them and formidable to tyrants only.

He has called together legislative bodies at places unusual, uncomfortable, and distant from the depository of their public Records, for the sole purpose of fatiguing them into compliance with his measures.

He has dissolved Representative Houses repeatedly, for opposing with manly firmness his invasions on the rights of the people.

He has refused for a long time, after such dissolutions, to cause others to be elected; whereby the Legislative powers, incapable of Annihilation, have returned to the People at large for their exercise; the State remaining in the mean time exposed to all the dangers of invasion from without, and convulsions within.

He has endeavoured to prevent the population of these States; for that purpose obstructing the Laws for Naturalization of Foreigners; refusing to pass others to encourage their migrations hither, and raising the conditions of new Appropriations of Lands.

He has obstructed the Administration of Justice, by refusing his Assent to Laws for establishing Judiciary powers.

He has made Judges dependent on his Will alone, for the tenure of their offices, and the amount and payment of their salaries.

He has erected a multitude of New Offices, and sent hither swarms of Officers to harrass our people, and eat out their substance.

He has kept among us, in times of peace, Standing Armies without the Consent of our legislatures.

He has affected to render the Military independent of and superior to the Civil power.

He has combined with others to subject us to a jurisdiction foreign to our constitution, and unacknowledged by our laws; giving his Assent to their Acts of pretended Legislation:

For Quartering large bodies of armed troops among us:

For protecting them, by a mock Trial, from punishment for any Murders which they should commit on the Inhabitants of these States:

For cutting off our Trade with all parts of the world:

For imposing Taxes on us without our Consent:

For depriving us in many cases, of the benefits of Trial by Jury:

For transporting us beyond Seas to be tried for pretended offences:

For abolishing the free System of English Laws in a

neighbouring Province, establishing therein an Arbitrary government, and enlarging its Boundaries so as to render it at once an example and fit instrument for introducing the same absolute rule into these Colonies:

For taking away our Charters, abolishing our most valuable Laws, and altering fundamentally the Forms of our Governments:

For suspending our own Legislatures, and declaring themselves invested with power to legislate for us in all cases whatsoever.

He has abdicated Government here, by declaring us out of his Protection and waging War against us.

He has plundered our seas, ravaged our Coasts, burnt our towns, and destroyed the lives of our people.

He is at this time transporting large Armies of foreign Mercenaries to compleat the works of death, desolation and tyranny, already begun with circumstances of Cruelty & perfidy scarcely paralleled in the most barbarous ages, and totally unworthy the Head of a civilized nation.

He has constrained our fellow Citizens taken Captive on the high Seas to bear Arms against their Country, to become the executioners of their friends and Brethren, or to fall themselves by their Hands.

He has excited domestic insurrections amongst us, and has endeavoured to bring on the inhabitants of our frontiers, the merciless Indian Savages, whose known rule of warfare, is an undistinguished destruction of all ages, sexes and conditions.

In every stage of these Oppressions We have Petitioned for Redress in the most humble terms: Our repeated Petitions have been answered only by repeated injury. A Prince whose character is thus marked by every act which may define a Tyrant, is unfit to be the ruler of a free people.

Nor have We been wanting in attentions to our Brittish brethren. We have warned them from time to time of attempts by their legislature to extend an unwarrantable jurisdiction over us. We have reminded them of the circumstances of our emigration and settlement here. We have appealed to their native justice and magnanimity, and we have conjured them by the ties of our common kindred to disavow these usurpations, which, would inevitably interrupt our connections and correspondence. They too have been deaf to the voice of justice and of consanguinity. We must, therefore, acquiesce in the necessity, which denounces our Separation, and hold them, as we hold the rest of mankind, Enemies in War, in Peace Friends.

We, therefore, the Representatives of the united States of America, in General Congress, Assembled, appealing to the Supreme Judge of the world for the rectitude of our intentions, do, in the Name, and by Authority of the good People of these Colonies, solemnly publish and declare, That these United Colonies are, and of Right ought to be Free and Independent States; that they are Absolved from all Allegiance to the British Crown, and that all political connection between them and the State of Great Britain, is and ought to be totally dissolved; and that as Free and Independent States, they have full Power to levy War, conclude Peace, contract Alliances, establish Commerce, and to do all other Acts and Things which Independent States may of right do. And for the support of this Declaration, with a firm reliance on the protection of divine Providence, we mutually pledge to each other our Lives, our Fortunes and our sacred Honor.

Georgia:
  Button Gwinnett
  Lyman Hall
  George Walton

North Carolina:
  William Hooper
  Joseph Hewes
  John Penn

South Carolina:
  Edward Rutledge
  Thomas Heyward, Jr.
  Thomas Lynch, Jr.
  Arthur Middleton

Massachusetts:
  John Hancock

Maryland:
  Samuel Chase
  William Paca
  Thomas Stone
  Charles Carroll of
  Carrollton

Virginia:
  George Wythe
  Richard Henry Lee
  Thomas Jefferson
  Benjamin Harrison
  Thomas Nelson, Jr.
  Francis Lightfoot Lee
  Carter Braxton

Pennsylvania:
  Robert Morris
  Benjamin Rush
  Benjamin Franklin
  John Morton
  George Clymer
  James Smith
  George Taylor
  James Wilson
  George Ross

Delaware:
  Caesar Rodney
  George Read
  Thomas McKean

New York:
William Floyd
Philip Livingston
Francis Lewis
Lewis Morris

New Jersey:
Richard Stockton
John Witherspoon
Francis Hopkinson
John Hart
Abraham Clark

New Hampshire:
Josiah Bartlett
William Whipple

Massachusetts:
Samuel Adams
John Adams
Robert Treat Paine
Elbridge Gerry

Rhode Island:
Stephen Hopkins
William Ellery

Connecticut:
Roger Sherman
Samuel Huntington
William Williams
Oliver Wolcott

New Hampshire:
Matthew Thornton

The Constitution of the United States of America

We the People of the United States, in Order to form a more perfect Union, establish Justice, insure domestic Tranquility, provide for the common defence, promote the general Welfare, and secure the Blessings of Liberty to ourselves and our Posterity, do ordain and establish this Constitution for the United States of America.

Article I - The Legislative Branch

Section 1 - The Legislature

All legislative Powers herein granted shall be vested in a Congress of the United States, which shall consist of a Senate and House of Representatives.

Section 2 - The House

The House of Representatives shall be composed of

Members chosen every second Year by the People of the several States, and the Electors in each State shall have the Qualifications requisite for Electors of the most numerous Branch of the State Legislature.

No Person shall be a Representative who shall not have attained to the Age of twenty five Years, and been seven Years a Citizen of the United States, and who shall not, when elected, be an Inhabitant of that State in which he shall be chosen.

[Representatives and direct Taxes shall be apportioned among the several States which may be included within this Union, according to their respective Numbers, which shall be determined by adding to the whole Number of free Persons, including those bound to Service for a Term of Years, and excluding Indians not taxed, three fifths of all other Persons.][1] The actual Enumeration shall be made within three Years after the first Meeting of the Congress of the United States, and within every subsequent Term of ten Years, in such Manner as they shall by Law direct. The Number of Representatives shall not exceed one for every thirty Thousand, but each State shall have at Least one Representative; and until such enumeration shall be made, the State of New Hampshire shall be entitled to chuse three, Massachusetts eight, Rhode Island and Providence Plantations one, Connecticut five, New York six, New Jersey four, Pennsylvania eight, Delaware one, Maryland six, Virginia ten, North Carolina five, South Carolina five and Georgia three.

When vacancies happen in the Representation from any

---

1. Changed by Section 2 of the Fourteenth Amendment.

State, the Executive Authority thereof shall issue Writs of Election to fill such Vacancies.

The House of Representatives shall chuse their Speaker and other Officers; and shall have the sole Power of Impeachment.

Section 3 - The Senate

The Senate of the United States shall be composed of two Senators from each State, [chosen by the Legislature thereof,][2] for six Years; and each Senator shall have one Vote.

Immediately after they shall be assembled in Consequence of the first Election, they shall be divided as equally as may be into three Classes. The Seats of the Senators of the first Class shall be vacated at the Expiration of the second Year, of the second Class at the Expiration of the fourth Year, and of the third Class at the Expiration of the sixth Year, so that one third may be chosen every second Year; [and if Vacancies happen by Resignation, or otherwise, during the Recess of the Legislature of any State, the Executive thereof may make temporary Appointments until the next Meeting of the Legislature, which shall then fill such Vacancies.][3]

No person shall be a Senator who shall not have attained to the Age of thirty Years, and been nine Years a Citizen of the United States, and who shall not, when elected, be an Inhabitant of that State for which he shall be chosen.

The Vice President of the United States shall be President of the Senate, but shall have no Vote, unless they be equally divided.

2. Changed by the Seventeenth Amendment.
3. Changed by the Seventeenth Amendment.

The Senate shall chuse their other Officers, and also a President pro tempore, in the Absence of the Vice President, or when he shall exercise the Office of President of the United States.

The Senate shall have the sole Power to try all Impeachments. When sitting for that Purpose, they shall be on Oath or Affirmation. When the President of the United States is tried, the Chief Justice shall preside: And no Person shall be convicted without the Concurrence of two thirds of the Members present.

Judgment in Cases of Impeachment shall not extend further than to removal from Office, and disqualification to hold and enjoy any Office of honor, Trust or Profit under the United States: but the Party convicted shall nevertheless be liable and subject to Indictment, Trial, Judgment and Punishment, according to Law.

Section 4 - Elections, Meetings

The Times, Places and Manner of holding Elections for Senators and Representatives, shall be prescribed in each State by the Legislature thereof; but the Congress may at any time by Law make or alter such Regulations, except as to the Places of Chusing Senators.

The Congress shall assemble at least once in every Year, and such Meeting shall be [on the first Monday in December,][4] unless they shall by Law appoint a different Day.

Section 5 - Membership, Rules, Journals, Adjournment

Each House shall be the Judge of the Elections, Returns

---

4. Changed by Section 2 of the Twentieth Amendment.

and Qualifications of its own Members, and a Majority of each shall constitute a Quorum to do Business; but a smaller number may adjourn from day to day, and may be authorized to compel the Attendance of absent Members, in such Manner, and under such Penalties as each House may provide.

Each House may determine the Rules of its Proceedings, punish its Members for disorderly Behaviour, and, with the Concurrence of two thirds, expel a Member.

Each House shall keep a Journal of its Proceedings, and from time to time publish the same, excepting such Parts as may in their Judgment require Secrecy; and the Yeas and Nays of the Members of either House on any question shall, at the Desire of one fifth of those Present, be entered on the Journal.

Neither House, during the Session of Congress, shall, without the Consent of the other, adjourn for more than three days, nor to any other Place than that in which the two Houses shall be sitting.

Section 6 - Compensation

[The Senators and Representatives shall receive a Compensation for their Services, to be ascertained by Law, and paid out of the Treasury of the United States.][5] They shall in all Cases, except Treason, Felony and Breach of the Peace, be privileged from Arrest during their Attendance at the Session of their respective Houses, and in going to and returning from the same; and for any Speech or Debate in either House, they shall not be questioned in any other Place.

---

5. Modified by the Twenty-Seventh Amendment.

No Senator or Representative shall, during the Time for which he was elected, be appointed to any civil Office under the Authority of the United States which shall have been created, or the Emoluments whereof shall have been increased during such time; and no Person holding any Office under the United States, shall be a Member of either House during his Continuance in Office.

Section 7 - Revenue Bills, Legislative Process, Presidential Veto

All bills for raising Revenue shall originate in the House of Representatives; but the Senate may propose or concur with Amendments as on other Bills.

Every Bill which shall have passed the House of Representatives and the Senate, shall, before it become a Law, be presented to the President of the United States; If he approve he shall sign it, but if not he shall return it, with his Objections to that House in which it shall have originated, who shall enter the Objections at large on their Journal, and proceed to reconsider it. If after such Reconsideration two thirds of that House shall agree to pass the Bill, it shall be sent, together with the Objections, to the other House, by which it shall likewise be reconsidered, and if approved by two thirds of that House, it shall become a Law. But in all such Cases the Votes of both Houses shall be determined by Yeas and Nays, and the Names of the Persons voting for and against the Bill shall be entered on the Journal of each House respectively. If any Bill shall not be returned by the President within ten Days (Sundays excepted) after it shall have been presented to him, the Same shall be a Law, in like Manner as if he had signed it, unless the Congress by their Adjournment prevent its Return, in which Case it shall not be a Law.

Every Order, Resolution, or Vote to which the Concurrence of the Senate and House of Representatives may be necessary (except on a question of Adjournment) shall be presented to the President of the United States; and before the Same shall take Effect, shall be approved by him, or being disapproved by him, shall be repassed by two thirds of the Senate and House of Representatives, according to the Rules and Limitations prescribed in the Case of a Bill.

Section 8 - Powers of Congress

The Congress shall have Power To lay and collect Taxes, Duties, Imposts and Excises, to pay the Debts and provide for the common Defence and general Welfare of the United States; but all Duties, Imposts and Excises shall be uniform throughout the United States;

To borrow money on the credit of the United States;

To regulate Commerce with foreign Nations, and among the several States, and with the Indian Tribes;

To establish an uniform Rule of Naturalization, and uniform Laws on the subject of Bankruptcies throughout the United States;

To coin Money, regulate the Value thereof, and of foreign Coin, and fix the Standard of Weights and Measures;

To provide for the Punishment of counterfeiting the Securities and current Coin of the United States;

To establish Post Offices and Post Roads;

To promote the Progress of Science and useful Arts, by

securing for limited Times to Authors and Inventors the exclusive Right to their respective Writings and Discoveries;

To constitute Tribunals inferior to the supreme Court;

To define and punish Piracies and Felonies committed on the high Seas, and Offenses against the Law of Nations;

To declare War, grant Letters of Marque and Reprisal, and make Rules concerning Captures on Land and Water;

To raise and support Armies, but no Appropriation of Money to that Use shall be for a longer Term than two Years;

To provide and maintain a Navy;

To make Rules for the Government and Regulation of the land and naval Forces;

To provide for calling forth the Militia to execute the Laws of the Union, suppress Insurrections and repel Invasions;

To provide for organizing, arming, and disciplining the Militia, and for governing such Part of them as may be employed in the Service of the United States, reserving to the States respectively, the Appointment of the Officers, and the Authority of training the Militia according to the discipline prescribed by Congress;

To exercise exclusive Legislation in all Cases whatsoever, over such District (not exceeding ten Miles square) as may, by Cession of particular States, and the acceptance of Congress, become the Seat of the Government of the United States, and to exercise like Authority over all Places purchased by the Consent of the Legislature of the State in which the Same shall be, for the Erection of Forts, Magazines, Arsenals, dock-Yards, and other needful Buildings; And

To make all Laws which shall be necessary and proper for carrying into Execution the foregoing Powers, and all other Powers vested by this Constitution in the Government of the United States, or in any Department or Officer thereof.

Section 9 - Limits on Congress

The Migration or Importation of such Persons as any of the States now existing shall think proper to admit, shall not be prohibited by the Congress prior to the Year one thousand eight hundred and eight, but a tax or duty may be imposed on such Importation, not exceeding ten dollars for each Person.

The privilege of the Writ of Habeas Corpus shall not be suspended, unless when in Cases of Rebellion or Invasion the public Safety may require it.

No Bill of Attainder or ex post facto Law shall be passed.

[No capitation, or other direct, Tax shall be laid, unless in Proportion to the Census or Enumeration herein before directed to be taken.][6]

No Tax or Duty shall be laid on Articles exported from any State.

No Preference shall be given by any Regulation of Commerce or Revenue to the Ports of one State over those of another: nor shall Vessels bound to, or from, one State, be obliged to enter, clear, or pay Duties in another.

No Money shall be drawn from the Treasury, but in Consequence of Appropriations made by Law; and a regular Statement and Account of the Receipts and Expenditures of all public Money shall be published from time to time.

No Title of Nobility shall be granted by the United States:

6. See Sixteenth Amendment.

And no Person holding any Office of Profit or Trust under them, shall, without the Consent of the Congress, accept of any present, Emolument, Office, or Title, of any kind whatever, from any King, Prince or foreign State.

Section 10 - Powers prohibited of States

No State shall enter into any Treaty, Alliance, or Confederation; grant Letters of Marque and Reprisal; coin Money; emit Bills of Credit; make any Thing but gold and silver Coin a Tender in Payment of Debts; pass any Bill of Attainder, ex post facto Law, or Law impairing the Obligation of Contracts, or grant any Title of Nobility.

No State shall, without the Consent of the Congress, lay any Imposts or Duties on Imports or Exports, except what may be absolutely necessary for executing it's inspection Laws: and the net Produce of all Duties and Imposts, laid by any State on Imports or Exports, shall be for the Use of the Treasury of the United States; and all such Laws shall be subject to the Revision and Controul of the Congress.

No State shall, without the Consent of Congress, lay any duty of Tonnage, keep Troops, or Ships of War in time of Peace, enter into any Agreement or Compact with another State, or with a foreign Power, or engage in War, unless actually invaded, or in such imminent Danger as will not admit of delay.

Article II - The Executive Branch Note

Section 1 - The President

The executive Power shall be vested in a President of the United States of America. He shall hold his Office during the

Term of four Years, and, together with the Vice-President chosen for the same Term, be elected, as follows:

Each State shall appoint, in such Manner as the Legislature thereof may direct, a Number of Electors, equal to the whole Number of Senators and Representatives to which the State may be entitled in the Congress: but no Senator or Representative, or Person holding an Office of Trust or Profit under the United States, shall be appointed an Elector.

[The Electors shall meet in their respective States, and vote by Ballot for two persons, of whom one at least shall not lie an Inhabitant of the same State with themselves. And they shall make a List of all the Persons voted for, and of the Number of Votes for each; which List they shall sign and certify, and transmit sealed to the Seat of the Government of the United States, directed to the President of the Senate. The President of the Senate shall, in the Presence of the Senate and House of Representatives, open all the Certificates, and the Votes shall then be counted. The Person having the greatest Number of Votes shall be the President, if such Number be a Majority of the whole Number of Electors appointed; and if there be more than one who have such Majority, and have an equal Number of Votes, then the House of Representatives shall immediately chuse by Ballot one of them for President; and if no Person have a Majority, then from the five highest on the List the said House shall in like Manner chuse the President. But in chusing the President, the Votes shall be taken by States, the Representation from each State having one Vote; a quorum for this Purpose shall consist of a Member or Members from two-thirds of the States, and a Majority of all the States shall be necessary to a Choice. In every Case, after the Choice of the President, the Person having the greatest Number of Votes of the Electors shall be the Vice President. But if there should remain two or more who have equal Votes, the Senate shall chuse from them by Ballot the Vice-President.][7]

The Congress may determine the Time of chusing the Electors, and the Day on which they shall give their Votes; which Day shall be the same throughout the United States.

No person except a natural born Citizen, or a Citizen of the United States, at the time of the Adoption of this Constitution, shall be eligible to the Office of President; neither shall any Person be eligible to that Office who shall not have attained to the Age of thirty-five Years, and been fourteen Years a Resident within the United States.

[In Case of the Removal of the President from Office, or of his Death, Resignation, or Inability to discharge the Powers and Duties of the said Office, the same shall devolve on the Vice President, and the Congress may by Law provide for the Case of Removal, Death, Resignation or Inability, both of the President and Vice President, declaring what Officer shall then act as President, and such Officer shall act accordingly, until the Disability be removed, or a President shall be elected.][8]

The President shall, at stated Times, receive for his Services, a Compensation, which shall neither be increased nor diminished during the Period for which he shall have been elected, and he shall not receive within that Period any

---

7. Changed by the Twelfth Amendment.
8. Changed by the Twentieth and Twenty-Fifth Amendments.

other Emolument from the United States, or any of them.

Before he enter on the Execution of his Office, he shall take the following Oath or Affirmation:

"I do solemnly swear (or affirm) that I will faithfully execute the Office of President of the United States, and will to the best of my Ability, preserve, protect and defend the Constitution of the United States."

Section 2 - Civilian Power over Military, Cabinet, Pardon Power, Appointments

The President shall be Commander in Chief of the Army and Navy of the United States, and of the Militia of the several States, when called into the actual Service of the United States; he may require the Opinion, in writing, of the principal Officer in each of the executive Departments, upon any subject relating to the Duties of their respective Offices, and he shall have Power to Grant Reprieves and Pardons for Offenses against the United States, except in Cases of Impeachment.

He shall have Power, by and with the Advice and Consent of the Senate, to make Treaties, provided two thirds of the Senators present concur; and he shall nominate, and by and with the Advice and Consent of the Senate, shall appoint Ambassadors, other public Ministers and Consuls, Judges of the supreme Court, and all other Officers of the United States, whose Appointments are not herein otherwise provided for, and which shall be established by Law: but the Congress may by Law vest the Appointment of such inferior Officers, as they think proper, in the President alone, in the Courts of Law, or in the Heads of Departments.

The President shall have Power to fill up all Vacancies that may happen during the Recess of the Senate, by granting Commissions which shall expire at the End of their next Session.

Section 3 - State of the Union, Convening Congress

He shall from time to time give to the Congress Information of the State of the Union, and recommend to their Consideration such Measures as he shall judge necessary and expedient; he may, on extraordinary Occasions, convene both Houses, or either of them, and in Case of Disagreement between them, with Respect to the Time of Adjournment, he may adjourn them to such Time as he shall think proper; he shall receive Ambassadors and other public Ministers; he shall take Care that the Laws be faithfully executed, and shall Commission all the Officers of the United States.

Section 4 - Disqualification

The President, Vice President and all civil Officers of the United States, shall be removed from Office on Impeachment for, and Conviction of, Treason, Bribery, or other high Crimes and Misdemeanors.

Article III - The Judicial Branch Note

Section 1 - Judicial powers

The judicial Power of the United States, shall be vested in one supreme Court, and in such inferior Courts as the Congress may from time to time ordain and establish. The Judges, both of the supreme and inferior Courts, shall hold their Offices during good Behavior, and shall, at stated Times, receive for their Services a Compensation which shall not be diminished during their Continuance in Office.

Section 2 - Trial by Jury, Original Jurisdiction, Jury Trials

The judicial Power shall extend to all Cases, in Law and Equity, arising under this Constitution, the Laws of the United States, and Treaties made, or which shall be made, under their Authority; to all Cases affecting Ambassadors, other public Ministers and Consuls; to all Cases of admiralty and maritime Jurisdiction; to Controversies to which the United States shall be a Party; to Controversies between two or more States; [between a State and Citizens of another State;][9] between Citizens of different States; between Citizens of the same State claiming Lands under Grants of different States, [and between a State, or the Citizens thereof, and foreign States, Citizens or Subjects.][10]

In all Cases affecting Ambassadors, other public Ministers and Consuls, and those in which a State shall be Party, the supreme Court shall have original Jurisdiction. In all the other Cases before mentioned, the supreme Court shall have appellate Jurisdiction, both as to Law and Fact, with such Exceptions, and under such Regulations as the Congress shall make.

The Trial of all Crimes, except in Cases of Impeachment, shall be by Jury; and such Trial shall be held in the State where the said Crimes shall have been committed; but when not committed within any State, the Trial shall be at such Place or Places as the Congress may by Law have directed.

---

9. Changed by the Eleventh Amendment.
10. Changed by the Eleventh Amendment.

Section 3 - Treason

Treason against the United States, shall consist only in levying War against them, or in adhering to their Enemies, giving them Aid and Comfort. No Person shall be convicted of Treason unless on the Testimony of two Witnesses to the same overt Act, or on Confession in open Court.

The Congress shall have power to declare the Punishment of Treason, but no Attainder of Treason shall work Corruption of Blood, or Forfeiture except during the Life of the Person attainted.

Article IV - The States
Section 1 - Each State to Honor all Others

Full Faith and Credit shall be given in each State to the public Acts, Records, and judicial Proceedings of every other State. And the Congress may by general Laws prescribe the Manner in which such Acts, Records and Proceedings shall be proved, and the Effect thereof.

Section 2 - State citizens, Extradition

The Citizens of each State shall be entitled to all Privileges and Immunities of Citizens in the several States.

A Person charged in any State with Treason, Felony, or other Crime, who shall flee from Justice, and be found in another State, shall on demand of the executive Authority of the State from which he fled, be delivered up, to be removed to the State having Jurisdiction of the Crime.

[No Person held to Service or Labour in one State, under the Laws thereof, escaping into another, shall, in Consequence of any Law or Regulation therein, be discharged from such Service or Labour, But shall be delivered up on Claim of the Party to whom such Service or Labour may be due.][11]

Section 3 - New States

New States may be admitted by the Congress into this Union; but no new States shall be formed or erected within the Jurisdiction of any other State; nor any State be formed by the Junction of two or more States, or parts of States, without the Consent of the Legislatures of the States concerned as well as of the Congress.

The Congress shall have Power to dispose of and make all needful Rules and Regulations respecting the Territory or other Property belonging to the United States; and nothing in this Constitution shall be so construed as to Prejudice any Claims of the United States, or of any particular State.

Section 4 - Republican government

The United States shall guarantee to every State in this Union a Republican Form of Government, and shall protect each of them against Invasion; and on Application of the Legislature, or of the Executive (when the Legislature cannot be convened) against domestic Violence.

Article V

The Congress, whenever two thirds of both Houses shall deem it necessary, shall propose Amendments to this Constitution, or, on the Application of the Legislatures of two thirds of the several States, shall call a Convention for

---

11. Changed by the Thirteenth Amendment.

proposing Amendments, which, in either Case, shall be valid to all Intents and Purposes, as part of this Constitution, when ratified by the Legislatures of three fourths of the several States, or by Conventions in three fourths thereof, as the one or the other Mode of Ratification may be proposed by the Congress; Provided that no Amendment which may be made prior to the Year One thousand eight hundred and eight shall in any Manner affect the first and fourth Clauses in the Ninth Section of the first Article; and that no State, without its Consent, shall be deprived of its equal Suffrage in the Senate.

Article VI - Debts, Supremacy, Oaths

All Debts contracted and Engagements entered into, before the Adoption of this Constitution, shall be as valid against the United States under this Constitution, as under the Confederation.

This Constitution, and the Laws of the United States which shall be made in Pursuance thereof; and all Treaties made, or which shall be made, under the Authority of the United States, shall be the supreme Law of the Land; and the Judges in every State shall be bound thereby, any Thing in the Constitution or Laws of any State to the Contrary notwithstanding.

The Senators and Representatives before mentioned, and the Members of the several State Legislatures, and all executive and judicial Officers, both of the United States and of the several States, shall be bound by Oath or Affirmation, to support this Constitution; but no religious Test shall ever be required as a Qualification to any Office or public Trust under the United States.

Article VII - Ratification Documents

The Ratification of the Conventions of nine States, shall be sufficient for the Establishment of this Constitution between the States so ratifying the Same.

Done in Convention by the Unanimous Consent of the States present the Seventeenth Day of September in the Year of our Lord one thousand seven hundred and Eighty seven and of the Independence of the United States of America the Twelfth. In Witness whereof We have hereunto subscribed our Names.

G. Washington - President and deputy from Virginia

New Hampshire:
John Langdon, Nicholas Gilman

Massachusetts:
Nathaniel Gorham, Rufus King

Connecticut:
Wm Saml Johnson, Roger Sherman

New York:
Alexander Hamilton

New Jersey:
Wil Livingston, David Brearley, Wm Paterson, Jona. Dayton

Pennsylvania:
B Franklin, Thomas Mifflin, Robt Morris, Geo. Clymer, Thos FitzSimons, Jared Ingersoll, James Wilson, Gouv Morris

Delaware:
Geo. Read, Gunning Bedford jun, John Dickinson, Richard Bassett, Jaco. Broom

Maryland:
James McHenry, Dan of St Tho Jenifer, Danl Carroll

Virginia:
John Blair, James Madison Jr.

North Carolina:
Wm Blount, Richd Dobbs Spaight, Hu Williamson

South Carolina:
J. Rutledge, Charles Cotesworth Pinckney, Charles Pinckney, Pierce Butler

Georgia:
William Few, Abr Baldwin

Attest: William Jackson, Secretary

Amendments to the U.S. Constitution

The following are the Amendments to the Constitution. The first ten Amendments collectively are commonly known as the Bill of Rights and were ratified effective December 15, 1791.

Amendment 1

Congress shall make no law respecting an establishment of religion, or prohibiting the free exercise thereof; or abridging the freedom of speech, or of the press; or the right of the people peaceably to assemble, and to petition the Government for a redress of grievances.

Amendment 2

A well regulated Militia, being necessary to the security of a free State, the right of the people to keep and bear Arms, shall not be infringed.

Amendment 3

No Soldier shall, in time of peace be quartered in any house, without the consent of the Owner, nor in time of war, but in a manner to be prescribed by law.

Amendment 4

The right of the people to be secure in their persons, houses, papers, and effects, against unreasonable searches and seizures, shall not be violated, and no Warrants shall issue, but upon probable cause, supported by Oath or affirmation, and particularly describing the place to be searched, and the persons or things to be seized.

Amendment 5

No person shall be held to answer for a capital, or otherwise infamous crime, unless on a presentment or indictment of a Grand Jury, except in cases arising in the land or naval forces, or in the Militia, when in actual service in time of War or public danger; nor shall any person be subject for the same offense to be twice put in jeopardy of life or limb; nor shall be compelled in any criminal case to be a witness against himself, nor be deprived of life, liberty, or property, without due process of law; nor shall private property be taken for public use, without just compensation.

Amendment 6

In all criminal prosecutions, the accused shall enjoy the right to a speedy and public trial, by an impartial jury of the State and district wherein the crime shall have been committed, which district shall have been previously ascertained by law, and to be informed of the nature and cause of the accusation; to be confronted with the witnesses against him; to have compulsory process for obtaining witnesses in his favor, and to have the Assistance of Counsel for his defence.

Amendment 7

In Suits at common law, where the value in controversy shall exceed twenty dollars, the right of trial by jury shall be preserved, and no fact tried by a jury, shall be otherwise re-examined in any Court of the United States, than according to the rules of the common law.

Amendment 8

Excessive bail shall not be required, nor excessive fines imposed, nor cruel and unusual punishments inflicted.

Amendment 9

The enumeration in the Constitution, of certain rights, shall not be construed to deny or disparage others retained by the people.

Amendment 10

The powers not delegated to the United States by the Constitution, nor prohibited by it to the States, are reserved to the States respectively, or to the people.

Amendment 11

Ratified February 7, 1795

The Judicial power of the United States shall not be construed to extend to any suit in law or equity, commenced or prosecuted against one of the United States by Citizens of another State, or by Citizens or Subjects of any Foreign State.

Amendment 12

Ratified June 15, 1804

The Electors shall meet in their respective states, and vote by ballot for President and Vice-President, one of whom, at least, shall not be an inhabitant of the same state with themselves; they shall name in their ballots the person voted for as President, and in distinct ballots the person voted for as Vice-President, and they shall make distinct lists of all persons voted for as President, and of all persons voted for as Vice-President and of the number of votes for each, which lists they shall sign and certify, and transmit sealed to the seat of the government of the United States, directed to the President of the Senate;

The President of the Senate shall, in the presence of the Senate and House of Representatives, open all the certificates and the votes shall then be counted;

The person having the greatest Number of votes for President, shall be the President, if such number be a majority of the whole number of Electors appointed; and if no person have such majority, then from the persons having the highest numbers not exceeding three on the list of those voted for as President, the House of Representatives shall choose immediately, by ballot, the President. But in choosing the President, the votes shall be taken by states, the representation from each state having one vote; a quorum for this purpose shall consist of a member or members from two-thirds of the states, and a majority of all the states shall be necessary to a choice. [And if the House of Representatives shall not choose a President whenever the right of choice shall devolve upon them, before the fourth day of March next following, then the Vice-President shall act as President, as in the case of the death or other constitutional disability of the President.][12]

The person having the greatest number of votes as Vice-President, shall be the Vice-President, if such number be a majority of the whole number of Electors appointed, and if no person have a majority, then from the two highest numbers on the list, the Senate shall choose the Vice-President; a quorum for the purpose shall consist of two-thirds of the whole number of Senators, and a majority of the whole number shall be necessary to a choice. But no person constitutionally ineligible to the office of President shall be eligible to that of Vice-President of the United States.

Amendment 13
Ratified December 6, 1865

Section 1. Neither slavery nor involuntary servitude, except as a punishment for crime whereof the party shall have been duly convicted, shall exist within the United States, or any place subject to their jurisdiction.

Section 2. Congress shall have power to enforce this article by appropriate legislation.

Amendment 14
Ratified July 9, 1868

Section 1. All persons born or naturalized in the United States, and subject to the jurisdiction thereof, are citizens of the United States and of the State wherein they reside. No State shall make or enforce any law which shall abridge the privileges or immunities of citizens of the United States; nor shall any State deprive any person of life, liberty, or property,

---

12. Superseded by Section 3 of the Twentieth Amendment.

without due process of law; nor deny to any person within its jurisdiction the equal protection of the laws.

Section 2. Representatives shall be apportioned among the several States according to their respective numbers, counting the whole number of persons in each State, excluding Indians not taxed. [But when the right to vote at any election for the choice of electors for President and Vice-President of the United States, Representatives in Congress, the Executive and Judicial officers of a State, or the members of the Legislature thereof, is denied to any of the male inhabitants of such State, being twenty-one years of age][13], and citizens of the United States, or in any way abridged, except for participation in rebellion, or other crime, the basis of representation therein shall be reduced in the proportion which the number of such male citizens shall bear to the whole number of male citizens twenty-one years of age in such State.

Section 3. No person shall be a Senator or Representative in Congress, or elector of President and Vice-President, or hold any office, civil or military, under the United States, or under any State, who, having previously taken an oath, as a member of Congress, or as an officer of the United States, or as a member of any State legislature, or as an executive or judicial officer of any State, to support the Constitution of the United States, shall have engaged in insurrection or rebellion against the same, or given aid or comfort to the enemies thereof. But Congress may by a vote of two-thirds of each House, remove such disability.

Section 4. The validity of the public debt of the United

---

13. Changed by Section 1 of the Twenty-Sixth Amendment.

States, authorized by law, including debts incurred for payment of pensions and bounties for services in suppressing insurrection or rebellion, shall not be questioned. But neither the United States nor any State shall assume or pay any debt or obligation incurred in aid of insurrection or rebellion against the United States, or any claim for the loss or emancipation of any slave; but all such debts, obligations and claims shall be held illegal and void.

Section 5. The Congress shall have power to enforce, by appropriate legislation, the provisions of this article.

Amendment 15
Ratified February 3, 1870

Section 1. The right of citizens of the United States to vote shall not be denied or abridged by the United States or by any State on account of race, color, or previous condition of servitude.

Section 2. The Congress shall have power to enforce this article by appropriate legislation.

Amendment 16
Ratified February 3, 1913

The Congress shall have power to lay and collect taxes on incomes, from whatever source derived, without apportionment among the several States, and without regard to any census or enumeration.

Amendment 17
Ratified April 8, 1913

The Senate of the United States shall be composed of two Senators from each State, elected by the people thereof, for six years; and each Senator shall have one vote. The electors in each State shall have the qualifications requisite for electors of the most numerous branch of the State legislatures.

When vacancies happen in the representation of any State in the Senate, the executive authority of such State shall issue writs of election to fill such vacancies: Provided, That the legislature of any State may empower the executive thereof to make temporary appointments until the people fill the vacancies by election as the legislature may direct.

This amendment shall not be so construed as to affect the election or term of any Senator chosen before it becomes valid as part of the Constitution.

Amendment 18
Ratified January 16, 1919

[**Section 1.** After one year from the ratification of this article the manufacture, sale, or transportation of intoxicating liquors within, the importation thereof into, or the exportation thereof from the United States and all territory subject to the jurisdiction thereof for beverage purposes is hereby prohibited.

Section 2. The Congress and the several States shall have concurrent power to enforce this article by appropriate legislation.

Section 3. This article shall be inoperative unless it shall have been ratified as an amendment to the Constitution by the legislatures of the several States, as provided in the Constitution, within seven years from the date of the submission hereof to the States by the Congress.][14]

14. Repealed by the Twenty-First Amendment.

Amendment 19

Ratified August 18, 1920

The right of citizens of the United States to vote shall not be denied or abridged by the United States or by any State on account of sex.

Congress shall have power to enforce this article by appropriate legislation.

Amendment 20

Ratified January 23, 1933

Section 1. The terms of the President and Vice President shall end at noon on the 20th day of January, and the terms of Senators and Representatives at noon on the 3d day of January, of the years in which such terms would have ended if this article had not been ratified; and the terms of their successors shall then begin.

Section 2. The Congress shall assemble at least once in every year, and such meeting shall begin at noon on the 3d day of January, unless they shall by law appoint a different day.

Section 3. If, at the time fixed for the beginning of the term of the President, the President elect shall have died, the Vice President elect shall become President. If a President shall not have been chosen before the time fixed for the beginning of his term, or if the President elect shall have failed to qualify, then the Vice President elect shall act as President until a President shall have qualified; and the Congress may by law provide for the case wherein neither a President elect nor a Vice President elect shall have qualified, declaring who shall then act as President, or the manner in which one who is to act shall be selected, and such person shall act accordingly until a President or Vice President shall have qualified.

Section 4. The Congress may by law provide for the case of the death of any of the persons from whom the House of Representatives may choose a President whenever the right of choice shall have devolved upon them, and for the case of the death of any of the persons from whom the Senate may choose a Vice President whenever the right of choice shall have devolved upon them.

Section 5. Sections 1 and 2 shall take effect on the 15th day of October following the ratification of this article.

Section 6. This article shall be inoperative unless it shall have been ratified as an amendment to the Constitution by the legislatures of three-fourths of the several States within seven years from the date of its submission.

Amendment 21
Ratified December 5, 1933

Section 1. The eighteenth article of amendment to the Constitution of the United States is hereby repealed.

Section 2. The transportation or importation into any State, Territory, or possession of the United States for delivery or use therein of intoxicating liquors, in violation of the laws thereof, is hereby prohibited.

Section 3. The article shall be inoperative unless it shall have been ratified as an amendment to the Constitution by conventions in the several States, as provided in the Constitution, within seven years from the date of the submission hereof to the States by the Congress.

Amendment 22
Ratified February 27, 1951

Section 1. No person shall be elected to the office of the President more than twice, and no person who has held the office of President, or acted as President, for more than two years of a term to which some other person was elected President shall be elected to the office of the President more than once. But this Article shall not apply to any person holding the office of President, when this Article was proposed by the Congress, and shall not prevent any person who may be holding the office of President, or acting as President, during the term within which this Article becomes operative from holding the office of President or acting as President during the remainder of such term.

Section 2. This article shall be inoperative unless it shall have been ratified as an amendment to the Constitution by the legislatures of three-fourths of the several States within seven years from the date of its submission to the States by the Congress.

Amendment 23
Ratified March 29, 1961

Section 1. The District constituting the seat of Government of the United States shall appoint in such manner as the Congress may direct: A number of electors of President and Vice President equal to the whole number of Senators and Representatives in Congress to which the District would be entitled if it were a State, but in no event more than the least populous State; they shall be in addition to those appointed by the States, but they shall be considered, for the purposes of the election of President and Vice President, to be electors appointed by a State; and they shall meet in the District and perform such duties as provided by the twelfth article of amendment.

Section 2. The Congress shall have power to enforce this article by appropriate legislation.

Amendment 24
Ratified January 23, 1964

Section 1. The right of citizens of the United States to vote in any primary or other election for President or Vice President, for electors for President or Vice President, or for Senator or Representative in Congress, shall not be denied or abridged by the United States or any State by reason of failure to pay any poll tax or other tax.

Section 2. The Congress shall have power to enforce this article by appropriate legislation.

Amendment 25
Ratified February 10, 1967

Section 1. In case of the removal of the President from office or of his death or resignation, the Vice President shall become President.

Section 2. Whenever there is a vacancy in the office of the Vice President, the President shall nominate a Vice President who shall take office upon confirmation by a majority vote of both Houses of Congress.

Section 3. Whenever the President transmits to the President pro tempore of the Senate and the Speaker of the House of Representatives his written declaration that he is unable to discharge the powers and duties of his office, and until he transmits to them a written declaration to the contrary, such powers and duties shall be discharged by the Vice President as Acting President.

Section 4. Whenever the Vice President and a majority of either the principal officers of the executive departments or of such other body as Congress may by law provide, transmit to the President pro tempore of the Senate and the Speaker of the House of Representatives their written declaration that the President is unable to discharge the powers and duties of his office, the Vice President shall immediately assume the powers and duties of the office as Acting President.

Thereafter, when the President transmits to the President pro tempore of the Senate and the Speaker of the House of Representatives his written declaration that no inability exists, he shall resume the powers and duties of his office unless the Vice President and a majority of either the principal officers of the executive department or of such other body as Congress may by law provide, transmit within four days to the President pro tempore of the Senate and the Speaker of the House of Representatives their written declaration that the President is unable to discharge the powers and duties of his office. Thereupon Congress shall decide the issue, assembling within forty eight hours for that purpose if not in session. If the Congress, within twenty one days after receipt of the latter written declaration, or, if Congress is not in session, within twenty one days after Congress is required to assemble, determines by two thirds vote of both Houses that the President is unable to discharge the powers and duties of his office, the Vice President shall continue to discharge the same as Acting President; otherwise, the President shall resume the powers and duties of his office.

Amendment 26
Ratified July 1, 1971

Section 1. The right of citizens of the United States, who are eighteen years of age or older, to vote shall not be denied or abridged by the United States or by any State on account of age.

Section 2. The Congress shall have power to enforce this article by appropriate legislation.

Amendment 27
Ratified May 7, 1992

No law, varying the compensation for the services of the Senators and Representatives, shall take effect, until an election of Representatives shall have intervened.

About the American Policy Roundtable & iVoters.com

A generation ago, a handful of "ordinary people" began meeting together out of a growing concern for America. Their conversations, prayers, and research led to the founding of an "extraordinary" public policy effort that would blossom into the American Policy Roundtable.

Recognizing that America is - at its core - a commitment to ideas and principles, the Roundtable was established with the mission of restoring the historic Judeo-Christian principles to American public policy. The Roundtable seeks to fulfill this mission statement by meeting three core objectives:

1) Rekindling the American Spirit -- by telling the story of Liberty everyday.
2) Building networks of leaders, who will help others join in the adventure of responsible citizenship.

3) Overcoming evil in civil society by promoting positive alternatives in public policy.

To accomplish these objectives the Roundtable model is built upon state-based public policy organizations, established in strategic states, all working to change America from "the bottom-up." Each state-based Roundtable organization serves under the auspices of the Board of Trustees of the American Policy Roundtable.

Impacting public policy is a process that requires multiple areas of activity. Competing in the realm of ideas is critical, but alone cannot prevail in a Constitutional Republic. Good government also requires constant vigilance in the legislative and judicial process as well as a constant flow of new leaders to serve in public office. The Roundtable model incorporates the necessity of this "three-pronged" approach to public policy.

Federal and state laws require certain types of organizations be established for these specific purposes. The Roundtable is a 501(c)3 education and research organization. Roundtable Freedom Forum is a 501(c)4 organization focused on legislative activity. The Liberty Committee is a non-affiliated federal PAC that works on selected candidate campaigns. Each of these three organizations are vital components in the state-based model pioneered by the Roundtable.

The American Policy Roundtable is an independent, nonpartisan, not-for-profit organization. No funds are solicited or accepted from any political parties or candidates.

LOG ON TO LEARN MORE

From MoveOutCongress.com
After the Tea Party©

Our Common History:

When the people of Boston grew tired of tyranny and abuse they supported the Boston Tea Party of 1773. When the party was over, the tyrannical party in power increased their oppression of Bostonians. In response, colonists stopped buying tea and other British imported products. John Adams himself joined in the resistance and stopped drinking tea. The colonists resisted British tyranny in every possible way. Three years later, colonial leaders meeting in Philadelphia signed the Declaration of Independence and threw off the rule of the British Parliament.

In 2009 millions of American supported protests called tea parties across the land. These protests, however, are not enough to enact true constitutional reforms in America. What is the next step? In the best tradition of American liberty it is once again time for a unified national resistance. This time

Americans must rise up together and bring constitutional accountability to the United States Congress.

Accountability to Congress? How on earth can citizens do that?

The formula is really quite simple. Americans refuse to support any member of Congress – until such time as that member proves their commitment to the Declaration of Independence and the U.S. Constitution as amended. The operative word in this formula is: proves. It is insufficient for any member of Congress to justify their positions solely on political affiliation. Prior voting record may be helpful but alone will not suffice. Labels such as "conservative" or "liberal" are not enough.

How will the resistance work?

1. All Americans who care about the future of the nation are urged to secure and read a copy of the Declaration of Independence and U.S. Constitution. A free online copy is available at www.aproundtable.org.

2. All Americans are urged to withdraw any form of support (other than prayer) from all members of Congress. This shall continue until such time as a member proves his/her genuine commitment to the Declaration of Independence and U.S. Constitution as amended. Criteria will include public statements and most importantly votes in Congress. Party affiliation is not considered as valid criteria.

3. MoveOutCongress.com and The Liberty Committee (an independent federal PAC) will publish a monthly update to let all Americans know which members of Congress have attempted to meet the above criteria. Citizens alone can decide for themselves if members of Congress have proven themselves worthy of future support.

4. The American Policy Roundtable and Roundtable Freedom Forum will host a series of events and media projects around the nation to encourage citizen leadership in MoveOutCongress.com.

That's it. The plan is simple and clear. Withdraw support for every member of Congress until they prove themselves worthy of your support. This is your right as an American. More than a right, this is our duty. Now is the time for all good men and women to put on their work clothes and come to the aid of their country - and fast.

Here is how to get started:

1. Download and read your copy of the Declaration of Independence and Constitution or order your print copy online.

2. Send your members of Congress their Termination Notices today. Hard copies go to district offices. Email versions go to D.C. offices.

3. Order your MoveOutCongress.com materials today and display them everywhere you go. Tell everyone who cares about America about MoveOutCongress.com.

4. Pay attention to regular email updates and keep sending

messages to your members of Congress and friends.

5. Make a contribution (if you can) to help spread the word across America. (This is a strictly non-profit project. All funds go right into the work.)

Sam Adams, the Father of the American Revolution, said it best:

"It does not require a majority to prevail, but rather an irate, tireless minority keen to set brush fires in people's minds."

It is time to rekindle the American spirit. Let us all rally to the Declaration and the Constitution and the principles upon which they stand!

For the sacred right of Liberty we now stand fast.

David Zanotti
President/CEO
The American Policy Roundtable
Roundtable Freedom Forum

Rob Walgate, *Vice-President, Roundtable and Freedom Forum*
Melanie Elsey, *National Legislative Director, American Policy Roundtable*
Dr. Jeff Sanders, *The Liberty Committee*
Dr. Sterling Glover, *Board of Trustees Roundtable and Freedom Forum*
Dr. Charles McGowen, *Medical Research Director, American Policy Roundtable*
Pastor John Bouquet, *Director, Shepherds Staff*

About The Liberty Committee

The Liberty Committee is a different kind of PAC. We are mostly volunteers and not ashamed to say so. Many of us have spent a lifetime of service in public policy or closely related fields, so we know first hand how "the game" is played. Except for us this is not a game.

The right to self-government is one of the self-evident truths described in the Declaration of Independence. The American experience of liberty under law exists because we have taken the responsibility of self-government seriously.

Part of that responsibility means serving our country. Few of us can serve or are welcome to serve in the U.S. military. Only one of 300 million Americans can sit in the White House at a time. But almost every one of us could either run for some public office, or volunteer and support someone gifted, trained and disciplined in the art of principled leadership. And everyone of us can contribute to an organization dedicated to bringing leaders into public office who will commit to principle over party – always.

The Liberty Committee is working to elect people to public office who will stand for the principles of the Declaration of Independence and the U.S. Constitution, regardless of their political affiliation.

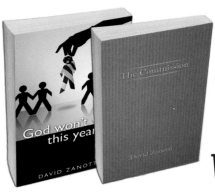

About *The Commission & God Won't Vote This Year*

"Dave Zanotti brings a wealth of hands-on experience and principled perspectives to bear in these insightful books. Worthwhile reads for anyone looking to make a difference in the world of politics."
- Michael Geer
President, Pennsylvania Family Institute

"If you are a thinking American who cares about the future of the nation - and if you're looking for solid, practical advice about what to do and how - then these books are for you."
- Dr. George Grant
Pastor, Parish Presbyterian Church
Chancellor, New College Franklin

"These books provide a solid understanding of the Biblical foundations for public policy. I suggest every Pastor read these books and preach from them."
- Dr. Sterling Glover
Academic Dean, Temple Theological Seminary

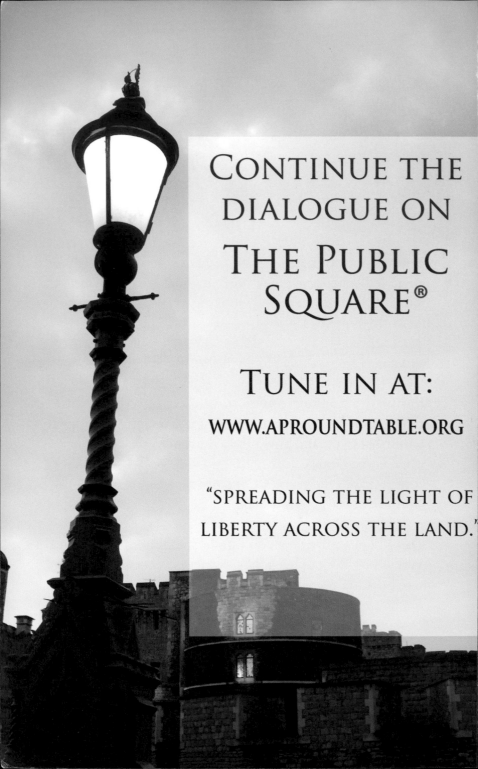

CONTINUE THE
DIALOGUE ON
THE PUBLIC
SQUARE®

TUNE IN AT:
WWW.APROUNDTABLE.ORG

"SPREADING THE LIGHT OF
LIBERTY ACROSS THE LAND."